RED PROPHET

The Punishing Intellectualism
of Vine Deloria Jr.

RED PROPHET

The Punishing Intellectualism
of Vine Deloria Jr.

DAVID E. WILKINS

FOREWORD BY BOBBY BRIDGER
AFTERWORD BY SAM SCINTA

FULCRUM

Library of Congress Cataloging-in-Publication Data

Names: Wilkins, David E. (David Eugene), 1954- author.
Title: Red prophet : the punishing intellectualism of Vine Deloria Jr. / written by David E. Wilkins.
Description: Golden, CO : Fulcrum Publishing, 2018. | Includes bibliographical references and index.
Identifiers: LCCN 2018013355 | ISBN 9781682751657
Subjects: LCSH: Deloria, Vine. | Indian authors--Biography. | Indian activists--Biography. | LCGFT: Biographies.
Classification: LCC E90.D45 W55 2018 | DDC 810.9/897--dc23
LC record available at https://lccn.loc.gov/2018013355

Printed in the United States of America
0 9 8 7 6 5 4 3 2 1

Cover: shield (artwork and photograph by Native Arts Trading); background (Shutterstock)

Fulcrum Publishing
4690 Table Mountain Dr., Ste. 100
Golden, CO 80403
800-992-2908 • 303-277-1623
fulcrum.bookstore.ipgbook.com

For Larry Leventhal, who fought tirelessly for Native treaty and human rights for more than forty years.

You are missed, Larry.

Contents

TABLES

FOREWORD

The first American Indian physician, Charles Eastman, wrote about medicine men and prophecy in 1911: "It is well-known that the American Indian had somehow developed occult power, and although in later days there have been many impostors, and allowing for the vanity and weakness of human nature, it is fair to assume that there must have been some even in the old days, yet there are well-attested instances of remarkable prophecies and other mystic practice."[1]

It is obvious that Dr. Eastman had to carefully phrase these remarks in order to accommodate those who would be eager to cast doubt on anything dealing with Indians—especially the "occult," prophecy, and Indians. He nonetheless skillfully continues for a full chapter in his book *The Soul of the Indian*, listing instances of Indian prophets and prophecies and, inspired by his genuine thirst for knowledge and a physician's passion for healing, urges an in-depth scientific study of the matter.

Vine Deloria Jr. obviously agreed with Dr. Eastman. Even though the multiple themes of Vine's body of work are intellectually broad, diverse, interdisciplinary, and, on the surface, secular, there was a profound spiritual keel unifying and guiding every one of his books, essays, speeches, and actions. Vine saw very early in his career that most of the problems facing modern American Indians were rooted in legal issues. Consequently, most of his early work was by necessity legal and secular. By the time *God Is Red* was published in 1973, however, Vine's spiritual side began to make itself more apparent, and toward the end of his life Vine increasingly opened up to reveal more of the mystic influences on his life and work. Beginning in 1999 with *Singing for a Spirit: A Portrait of the Dakota Sioux*, in which he shared the impact of Dakota prophecy on his own family's rich spiritual heritage, Vine offered a glimpse that suggested more of the powerful unseen forces that had been directing him all along. Vine departed on his spirit journey November 13, 2005, shortly after delivering his final edits for *The World We Used to Live In: Remembering the Powers of the Medicine Men*, in which he explored in depth the very topic of the American Indian's gift of prophecy that Dr. Eastman had called for ninety-four years earlier. Powerfully complementing this mystical direction, Vine's celebrated historian son, Philip, and noted Jungian scholar Jerome S. Bernstein also did an extraordinary job editing Vine's unfinished manuscript, and in 2009 the posthumously published *C. G. Jung and the Sioux Traditions: Dreams, Visions, Nature, and the Primitive* offered even more insight into the metaphysical nature of Vine's perspectives. Because the life course of four generations of the Deloria family was set in motion in Dakota prophecy more than a half century *before* Dr. Eastman called for scientific research into the Indigenous gift of prescient awareness in 1911, *prophecy* is truly the essential place to begin David Wilkins's splendid analytical biography, *Red Prophet: The Punishing Intellectualism of Vine Deloria Jr.*

After extended genealogical research into several versions of the family name in various parts of the country, Vine, as usual, gravitated to the oral tradition and simply retold his father's account of their family's incredible story in *Singing for a Spirit: A Portrait of the Dakota Sioux*. According to the Reverend Vine Deloria Sr., Vine's paternal great-great-grandfather was a French Huguenot orphan. Arriving in North America from France around 1750 to avoid religious persecution, circumstance deposited young François with a fur-trapping expedition on the Great Plains in his late teens. One day François and another young man were assigned the task of retrieving some lost horses. When the pair returned with their ponies, they discovered their entire trapping party had been massacred. Suddenly, they were alone on the prairie without provisions. Attempting to find their way back to the nearest community, the young men quickly became lost, and after a while François's companion died of starvation. François was near death himself when he was discovered, nursed to health, and adopted by the Yanktonai Dakota. François eventually married a young Dakota woman, and they had three children, among them a son born in 1816, also named François. Unable to pronounce François, the Sioux called both father and son *Saswe*. The younger Saswe lived his entire life in Dakota culture and rose to become a very powerful Yanktonai Dakota medicine man. Saswe was fifteen and just beginning on his path as a medicine man when the famous Hunkpapa medicine man and mystic warrior Sitting Bull was born in 1831. The pair certainly came to know each other, as the Yanktonai frequently aligned themselves with the Hunkpapa, Two Kettles, and Blackfeet bands of Teton Sioux, and all of them called the Standing Rock region home.

When he entered his teenage years, the younger Saswe began occasionally hearing voices calling his name, which led him to discuss the unusual occurrence with tribal medicine men. The elders wisely suggested an organized vision quest for young Saswe. Many sacred powers and instructions for uses of sacred talismans were presented to Saswe during the experience, but the centerpiece of the vision was a road leading into a black tipi. Once inside the lodge, Saswe immediately discovered he could not turn and leave; his only option was the choice of traveling one of two roads in the lodge. One was "chalky-white" with four skeletons positioned as if pondering the road. Beside the skeletons were stacked bundles of grass. The second road was "blood red" with four purification lodges placed at strategic locations along the way. Saswe chose the blood-red road.

Afterward, medicine men interpreted the vision and informed Saswe that if had selected the white road, four generations of his descendants would have enjoyed safe, prosperous lives. Nevertheless, they would contribute little, if any, spiritual value to the world. In choosing the red road, however, Saswe had selected the spiritual path. Yet the red road was also one of danger. The repetition of the number 4 in the vision was an indication to the medicine men that Saswe would kill four members of his own tribe, and the four purification lodges represented his quest in the future for redemption. Significantly, the four lodges and Saswe's decision to follow the red road also committed four generations of the Deloria family to that same spiritual path.

Saswe eventually did kill four Indian men. Each of the killings was a complicated tribal matter, sanctioned within the tribe and thus justified, yet they still haunted Saswe for the rest of his life. After many decades of healing people as a traditional Dakota medicine man, Saswe eventually sought the spiritual advice of Episcopal priests to heal himself, and they converted him to Christianity. Later, Saswe's son—Vine's grandfather—Tipi Sapa/ Philip, became one of only a handful of the very first Sioux Episcopal priests. Philip's son, Vine Sr., became South Dakota's first Sioux Episcopal archbishop. Continuing in the tradition, in the 1970s *Time* magazine referred to Vine Deloria Jr. as "one of the ten most important religious thinkers of the 20th century"; it was equally significant at the time of his walking on, however, that he was profoundly respected and referred to throughout Indian country with great reverence simply as "Uncle Vine."

So it is poetic and appropriate that David Wilkins titled his book *Red Prophet: The Punishing Intellectualism of Vine Deloria Jr.* And it is also important academically that a scholar with David's unique insights and talent has successfully written the very first biography of Vine Deloria Jr. with the daunting mission of chronicling his life while simultaneously analyzing and categorizing his extraordinary body of work. Significantly, as tumultuous global, social, political, and environmental change is looming in the coming decades, I believe *Red Prophet: The Punishing Intellectualism of Vine Deloria Jr.* is destined to become a trusted guide for those venturing into Vine's body of work seeking both Indigenous and non-Indigenous political, ecological, and organizational answers and solutions.

David is truly a personification of Vine's work in action. He and Vine were friends for twenty-five years, beginning when Vine recognized something special in David soon after they met. At the time of their meeting, Vine was the leading advocate for the recognition of the sovereignty of David's nation, the Lumbee Tribe of North Carolina. Later, Vine recruited David to the University of Arizona, where as a professor of law and political science Vine was developing a program that would evolve into the first master of arts degree in the country offered in American Indian studies. David eventually coauthored two important legal books with Vine: *Tribes, Treaties, and Constitutional Tribulations*, and *The Legal Universe: Observations of the Foundation of American Law*.

But it is also meaningful that David wrote this biography because he personally represents the embodiment of three important cornerstones of Vine's work: (1) Tribal Sovereignty, (2) Self-Determination, and (3) Environmental Sacredness. The story of David's youth is one of the recovery of personal tribal identity that also leads to recognition of his nation's sovereignty. David's own history is also a splendid example of rising above the insidious, federally imposed "termination" Indian policies of the mid-twentieth century and becoming a highly respected scholar, professor, and authority on the policy of Indian self-determination in the process. And, finally, David's writing transcends the boundary of "Indian–non-Indian" stereotypes to logically and eloquently articulate multiple interdisciplinary social, political, and religious problems, all the while remaining personally rooted in a sense of what is sacred.

A sacred sense of place has certainly prevailed at Standing Rock since before the time of Saswe and Sitting Bull, forward to the unprecedented contributions by Vine Deloria Jr. to our continuing efforts to understand the nearly 600 hundred years of our troubled relationship as Indigenous and non-Indigenous North Americans. On a personal level, as a non-Indian, from our first handshake a silent sense of the sacred certainly permeated my thirty-year friendship with Vine Deloria Jr. And our first meeting was indeed mystical: Soon after I finished reading *God Is Red*, my wife and I were en route to Denver to record my epic ballad *Seekers of the Fleece*, and I very earnestly said to her that I *wished* I could somehow meet Vine Deloria Jr. Two days later, I met him. After a brief introduction, I performed my Lakota ballad that is based on the meeting of Lakota holy man Black Elk and the poet John Neihardt and their book, *Black Elk Speaks*, and Vine immediately invited me to dinner to talk. The moment we first chatted it was like we had been friends forever, but for more than three decades of conversations we rarely, if ever, discussed so-called past life memories or the topic of reincarnation except in the most superficial terms. We were simply friends. Early in the friendship when my rational mind questioned why this very powerful Dakota philosopher chose me as his close friend, I reasoned that he was always attracted to underdogs, endoheretics, and anyone creating the hybrid forms of thinking necessary to get outside of the box, and I most surely fit that description.

From that initial meeting until he walked on, however, this powerful *sense* that we were *meant* to be best friends prevailed. The fact that he was Dakota and I was non-Indian made no difference at all; it was unspoken and accepted by both of us. Indeed, Vine's wife, Barbara, and their children also seemed to understand our relationship as *family*, and there was no need to confuse it by analyzing things. And the warm feeling of family still lives on between Barb, Phil, Dan, and Jeanne and my family. What I do understand and can explain about such things is that Vine *truly* loved music the same way I—and most musicians—truly love music. And I know that my music made him happy and brought even more joy, music, and laughter into his and his family's life, and there is profound sacredness in loving anything like that. So Vine and his family taught me that sacredness often begins mystically and slowly ages and deepens until it becomes "normal."

Increasingly, I remembered moments with Vine and his family as the numbers of Water Protectors steadily grew at the recent gathering at Standing Rock. As the encampment there swelled and the drama entered global mainstream media, I often wondered about the prophecies of Saswe. But I also thought much about the reunification prophecies of Lakota holy man Black Elk, whose story somehow initially brought me to meet Vine and his family. The formidable foundation of legal, religious, social, and philosophical tactics in Vine's books often could be heard clearly in the Protectors' language when they spoke to television news journalists or in videos calling for assistance. The Water Protectors gathering under the single banner of "Save the Sacred" especially echoed Vine's years of writing of the sacredness of space throughout his oeuvre and implied his profound impact upon the thinking of both modern Indian and non-Indian environmentalists; indeed, the unification of Indian and non-Indian environmentalists at Standing Rock certainly represents the first major meeting and bonding of these two powerful groups, and now they stand together armed with Vine's legacy concerning treaty rights, tribal sovereignty, Indigenous self-determinism, and the legality of sacredness.

Vine's last books *Singing for a Spirit* and *The World We Used to Live In*, and the posthumously published *C. G. Jung and the Sioux Traditions* certainly fulfilled Dr. Charles Eastman's call for deeper examination of the American Indian's prophetic insights. Perhaps we will all learn even more about the American Indian gift of prophecy and a sense of the sacredness of place as the drama at Standing Rock and elsewhere in America continues to unfold in the days to come. Fortunately, we now have David Wilkins's *Red Prophet: The Punishing Intellectualism of Vine Deloria Jr.* to guide us on our journey to understand the increasingly vital legacy of Vine Deloria Jr.

—*Bobby Bridger*

PREFACE

In January 2005, just a few months before he walked on, Vine Deloria Jr. became the second recipient of the American Indian Visionary Award tendered by *Indian Country Today*, the leading Native news organization. He was proud of this recognition, and although he never said as much, I believe he actually preferred being the *second* rather than the first person to receive this honor.

Why? Because Deloria, with his unparalleled activist and scholarly career, always felt he worked somewhat at a distance from the originating source of true sovereignty. Thus, he held the deepest respect for individuals such as the first Visionary Award recipient, his friend, the late Billy Frank Jr. (Nisqually), a man who clearly embodied the natural sovereignty that emanates from living within, depending on, and tirelessly defending sacred lands, waterways, and the species connected to them. Deloria felt that strong, resolute Native people like Billy were most deserving of such recognition.

Most of Deloria's adult life was spent in unrelenting, prodigious, and largely successful efforts to provide grounded Native individuals and their governments with the intellectual, theoretical, philosophical, and substantive arguments necessary to support their inherent personal and national sovereignty. His work with Billy Frank Jr. and brilliant Native strategist Hank Adams (Assiniboine) during the famous "Fish Wars" of the 1970s, which culminated in the treaty-affirming *Boldt* decision, perfectly exemplified the powerful partnerships that should exist between academics and activists. Deloria was keenly aware that this em-

brace of full-throttle sovereignty was the foundation for meaningful nation-to-nation and intergovernmental relationships, both
of and between Native nations, and between Native nations and
non-Native governments at all levels.

Deloria was undeniably one of the most prolific Indigenous
writers in history. He authored, coauthored, edited, and coedited
nearly 30 books, more than 200 articles and essays, and delivered
an untold number of keynotes, lectures, interviews, and congressional testimonials. Equally as impressive as his scholarly output
was the range of intellectual disciplines he traversed with aplomb,
including work encompassing law, religion and theology, natural
and social sciences, literary criticism, education, anthropology,
paleontology, philosophy, and political science.

He also held important positions outside the Academy, heading the National Congress of American Indians (NCAI) in the
1960s, and serving on many boards. He played a leading role in
developing and leading critically important organizations such as
the Institute for the Development of Indian Law, which he founded, and others that sought to improve the quality of life for Natives and non-Natives. Now, more than ten years after his death,
he has become an iconic figure, something that would have both
unsettled and amused him.

To me, Deloria was much more than the sum of his public
accomplishments. For twenty-five years he was my mentor and
my friend, helping to shape me into a scholar and a responsible
human being. His personal influence for me began with his recognition of and advocacy for my nation—the Lumbee of North
Carolina. He and his aunt, the noted ethnographer and linguist
Ella Deloria, studied and supported our people beginning in the
1940s, at a time when other national Native figures and organizations disparaged the Lumbee and our efforts to acquire full federal
recognition.

Our paths first crossed in a sustained way in 1980 because of
his work with the Lumbee Nation. Deloria had long been friends
with the late Helen Maynor Scheirbeck (Lumbee), who was her-
self a brilliant strategist who worked tirelessly on behalf of Native peoples. At Helen's recommendation, Deloria recruited me
to a new MA degree program he had developed at the University

of Arizona, a two-year terminal degree in political science that focused on training Native students in the quirks, contradictions, and nuances of federal Indian policy and law.

I became part of a small cohort of Native students, thrilled at the possibility of studying with a man we affectionately, and with some trepidation, referred to as "the Godfather" of Native politics, policy, and law. We jokingly called ourselves "Vine's Disciples," but there was an element of truth to this moniker because we were aware of our profound privilege and opportunity to study with the most gifted intellectual of our time. Each of us was ready to learn and accept what was required in order to become active and informed defenders of Indigenous nationhood.

Vine had a pedagogical style all his own—a combination of acrid wit, biting commentary, and relentless questioning. Many found his methods domineering, but, if you could get past the curmudgeonly, off-putting exterior and prove your serious intent to learn, he was a generous teacher, giving time and sincere consideration on how to identify and hone each person's unique skills. Those who finished this intellectually rich and rigorous program left feeling prepared to engage our nations on multiple fronts, armed with research and writing skills that would enable us to continue to mature in our chosen fields. He exercised a profound influence on all those he loved, mercilessly critiqued, and chose to strategize with.

My relationship with him and his wife, Barbara, an impressive intellect in her own right, broadened and deepened over the ensuing decades. While he would always remain my mentor, we also became good friends, and I had the honor of coauthoring two books with him.[2]

In August 1994, just after I lost my father, Vine wrote a letter that touched me deeply, expressing his condolences and sharing some of his own heartfelt feelings about death and the afterlife. He conveyed a sense of compassion and kindness he rarely displayed in public. My grief had been made worse by the fact that Dad passed on the day before I managed to get home to North Carolina to say good-bye; "Don't grieve that you didn't make it back home in time to see your dad," he wrote, "people often feel they have accomplished their life's work and don't want their close ones to go through the experience of watching them die—birth and death are often quite solitary things."

He went on to say that

> it will take a long time to get over it. I still have flash-backs about my folks and I suppose that it lasts the rest of your life. They were always there waiting to take you in and after they are both gone you just keep looking around and feel kind of exposed to the world…. You finally come to realize that you are providing the same kind of security for your kids and that your folks, right up to the present, were probably still remembering their parents and looking around to see where they are. Maybe that is the nature of life on earth.[3]

He then moved into deeper reflections about life and what, if anything, lies beyond. Death, he said, forces you "to ask yourself the question of what life is after everything is said and done. You remember the good times and think about the struggles your parents had to raise a family and then you begin to wonder if any-thing has any permanence." He surmised,

> Here is where I think that churches go wrong by hy-pothesizing some kind of artificial afterlife based on some kind of moral accomplishments achieved by fol-lowing their rules. There is good and bad in everyone—a lot of thoughtlessness by everyone—and plenty of missed opportunities and misunderstandings. So what-ever judgment there is can't actually be too hard and I suspect that people move right along with another phase of cosmic life.[4]

Finally, he shared with me a sense of his own inevitable mor-tality: "Deaths really shake me up anymore because I know I have spent the majority of my allotted time already and I have a lot of things undone—with each death of people around me a lot of possibilities are simply foreclosed." Ever the pragmatist, he con-cluded by observing,

You have to accept that and try to do things that count. But earning a living and taking care of your family takes a lot of time and energy. I will stop being so depressing except that I remember too well all the feelings I had when my folks died a few years back and I suspect you are having the same kind of shock and emptiness so I just wanted you to know that your disorientation is real and everyone who is at all sensitive to the situation feels the part of them that is not missing.[5]

In July 2004, I sent him a draft essay that identified and expanded upon many of the innovative ideas and suggested reforms he had proposed for both Native and non-Native audiences during his public life. That essay would later be included in the collection that Steve Pavlik and Daniel Wildcat published in 2006 titled *Destroying Dogma: Vine Deloria Jr. and His Influence on American Society*. Vine returned my draft a few months later with an accompanying letter. He said, "I had read your article on my way to work yesterday as I was clearing out part of my files. It really is a major piece of scholarship and mind-reading on your part." He went on, "It occurred to me that after I'm gone—and people my age have to think in those terms—that you could keep the article and update it, add a few well-chosen sentences from our correspondence and have yourself a nice quick book."[6]

Deloria's sense of timing, especially about publications, was impeccable, and I always took to heart his suggestions. Others have written essays that provide biographical details about his life,[7] and Deloria wrote a detailed family genealogy that wonderfully covered the history of the Deloria family back to the 1750s in *Singing for a Spirit: A Portrait of the Dakota Sioux*.[8] But little scholarship has been produced that focuses on his philosophical, political, legal, cultural, and economic recommendations for reform. This short book looks to provide that important data within a context and format suggested by Deloria himself.

As Western science finally begins to catch up with the knowledge long held by Indigenous peoples; as there appears to be a dawning, broad understanding that there is no boundary between us, the earth, and other creatures; as we defend water and life in places like Vine's home at Standing Rock, I grieve that he is not here to guide our actions, to sharpen our minds—I worry that we have arrived too late.

And yet, I still hear Vine's voice—simultaneously mocking and encouraging, hopeful and cynical, caustic and kindly—admonishing me just as he did in so many jarring, middle-of-the-night phone calls, *"Wilkins! Did you hear about what's going on? You need to write about it!"* I am reminded that, although he has walked on, Vine Deloria Jr. left a legacy of ideas that will help our world survive through these dangerous times. His words still comfort and inspire, *"You have to accept that and try to do things that count."*

The blazing, cantankerous prophet continues to illuminate the path.

Acknowledgments

I am deeply grateful for the inspiration, love, and outstanding editorial skills of my wife, Shelly Hulse Wilkins, who took my rough-hewn manuscript and strengthened and clarified it with her impeccable writing skills. I am delighted to be walking this road with her by my side.

Writing this book has been both a professional and deeply personal endeavor. A great deal of the material used came from my own correspondence with Vine and from his personal files, which Barbara Deloria was kind enough to open to me after he walked on. I am also thankful to Bobby Bridger and Sam Scinta, both dear friends to me and Vine. Each has used their considerable talents—Bobby as a musician and playwright and Sam as a writer and publisher—to benefit Native peoples and issues. Norbert Hill, Vine's close friend and colleague also deserves special appreciation, as he was committed to this project from the very beginning.

Finally, to young friends, Gabriel Duenes, a good neighbor for several years, and Elise Hui, whose wry perspective on the state of the world, bagels, and table tennis is wise and amusing. They, along with my grandsons, Kai and Levi, give me great hope for the future and the realization of Vine's vison for a better world populated by truly mature human beings.

Chapter 1

Eyes Wide Open

Politics of Activism Infused by Reflective, Responsible Sovereignty

Vine Victor Deloria Jr., a Yankton by blood, was born in Martin, South Dakota, on March 26, 1933. He was the first of three children that his father, Vine V. Deloria Sr., and his mother, Barbara S. Eastburn Deloria, would bring into the world. His father and grandfather, Philip J. Deloria (Tipi Sapa), Standing Rock Lakota citizens, were both Episcopal priests. He grew up in Martin, a small border town next to the Pine Ridge Reservation where his father was doing missionary work.[9]

His grandfather, Philip, was the son of the well-known Yankton chief, François (Saswe) des Lauriers. Saswe, a powerful holy man in the Lakota tradition, was a signer of the 1858 accord with the United States by which the Lakota ceded a great deal of territory in southeastern South Dakota in exchange for retention of their reduced lands and other vital rights and benefits along the Missouri River.[10] Throughout his life, Saswe had a series of visions and life experiences that would impact generations of his family's vocational and religious choices, culminating in a very active presence in the Episcopal Church well into the late twentieth century.[11] His visions guided his decision to direct his son to become a Christian and a priest.

As the son of a prominent priest, Vine Deloria Jr. traveled frequently with his father in Indian Country and attended both church services and traditional tribal events. One of his most lasting and formative boyhood memories was of a visit to the site of the 1890 Wounded Knee Massacre. He recalled seeing some of the survivors of that horrific event on the reservation during his childhood.[12]

Vine attended an off-reservation school in Martin before heading out in 1949 as a sixteen-year-old to attend Kent School, a private college-prep institution in Connecticut. Deloria graduated in 1951 and then enrolled at the Colorado School of Mines in Golden, Colorado, with the goal of becoming a geologist. In 1952 in an application for a John Whitney Foundation educational grant, he wrote that his plan was to earn a degree in geological engineering because "our country needs geologists very badly … I have a very deep feeling for the land since my ancestors, the Sioux Indians, once ruled it." "My ultimate purpose," he said, "is to become a good geologist. Then I would like to remain in South Dakota to help build up the state, particularly the immense tracts of land held by the Indians."[13]

Deloria elaborated further, indicating the early primacy of land in his consciousness:

> There are many Indian ministers, teachers, government workers, and so on. But I know there is a great need for a geologist, who is himself an Indian and naturally has a keen interest in the welfare of the Indians. For example, I know that the average Sioux Indian in South Dakota has very little conception of mineral deposits which might be underneath the very ground he owns. I would like, not only to locate such deposits, but also enlighten the owners so that they will stop selling their lands so cheaply.[14]

While seemingly deeply committed to the study of geology, he flunked out of school upon the realization that he was not meant to be a "rockhound." He then briefly attended Iowa State College in Ames, but found himself uninspired by that as well. He decided to enlist in the US Marine Corps, where he was trained as a telephone repairman and honorably served from 1954 to 1956. Deloria always recalled his military years with affection.

Financial support from the GI bill enabled him to return to Iowa State College, and it was there that he met his future wife, Barbara Jeanne Nystrom.[15] They graduated and married on the same day in 1958. Together, they had three children: Philip, Daniel, and Jeanne.

The next three years were unsettled. Deloria attended graduate school at the University of Oregon for time, but money was short, so he and Barbara decided to move to Rock Island, Illinois, where he worked in a machine shop for a year before he enrolled in the Lutheran School of Theology in Chicago. In 1960, he and his family moved again, this time to Puerto Rico where he taught English at Colegio San Justo, an Episcopal boarding school close to San Juan, but that endeavor "blew up after three months," and he returned to Lutheran Seminary where he earned a master's degree in 1963.[16]

He then went to work with the United Scholarship Service in Denver. A little more than a year later his career would again take a dramatic shift when at the age of thirty-one he became the executive director of the National Congress of American Indians (NCAI), the country's leading Native interest group. Three years at NCAI provided Vine the opportunity to learn firsthand about the major issues, hopes, and concerns of Indigenous people throughout the United States.

By the end of his term, he understood that a law degree was necessary if he hoped to tackle critical issues such as defense of treaty rights, land reacquisition, empowerment of Native government self-determination, and recovery and revitalization of the concept of tribal sovereignty.

Custer Awakens!

When he applied to law school, Deloria had letters of recommendation from US senator Karl Mundt of South Dakota, Robert

L. Rosenthal of the United Scholarship Service (where he had served as a field representative before being elected to the NCAI), and Jack Greenberg, director of the NAACP's Legal Defense and Educational Fund. Rosenthal's letter was the most personal. He wrote that he had come to know Deloria well over the years. "He was young and new and naïve in the field of Indian affairs when he began work for USS," said Rosenthal. But, he continued, "he is now well versed in this field as an independent scholar, and he has accomplished this self-education while on the job, developing a strong organization and serving as administrator, fund-raiser, and coordinator of a wide variety of activities."[17]

Deloria entered the University of Colorado Law School in 1967 and received his JD in 1970. Undertaking three years of law school while raising a family would have been enough for most people, but during those years he also worked directly with several Native nations and organizations, including the Mohawk Tribe of the Caughnawaga Reserve in Quebec, Canada, and several Native peoples in Nevada and South Dakota. He served on a committee to deal with the complications associated with the Alcatraz Takeover off the coast of San Francisco, and was on several national boards, including the Council of Indian Affairs, the Board of Inquiry into Hunger and Malnutrition, the National Office for the Rights of the Indigent, the Committee on Indian Work, the Executive Council of the Episcopal Church, and the Southwest Intergroup Council.

Perhaps most impressively, it was during this period that he wrote his first and best-selling book, *Custer Died for Your Sins: An Indian Manifesto*. It was published in 1969, the year *before* he graduated from law school. *Custer*, of course, catapulted his name and, more importantly, his visionary intellectual ideas, into the public arena at a time of social upheaval and questioning. It would inspire a generation to consider the human and civil rights of Native peoples, and its concepts resonate today.

Long before the word *decolonization* became ubiquitous, Deloria, in *Custer*, advocated for Red Power, the bold assertion that Indigenous peoples can speak, think, and act for themselves. He rejected federal paternalistic policies and demanded that church leaders, anthropologists, and other so-called Indian experts leave

Native peoples alone and show respect for Indigenous self-determination and diversity.

He also warned Native peoples about the pitfalls of mimicking the political and social movement strategies used by other groups legitimately seeking to exercise and define their rights within the United States. For example, some Natives were copying methods and ideologies employed by African Americans rallying for Black Power. While Deloria supported the efforts of this movement, he felt strongly that Indians had unique concerns that should not be simplified or subsumed by others. "I refuse," said Deloria, "to do the Indian thing in a black context."[18]

Custer was reviewed positively by Natives and critics alike, but some academics—most notably anthropologists, the recipients of a full chapter of biting criticism—felt maligned. Some wrote Deloria directly to express their concerns, and in August 1969, he responded to one such letter from anthropologist George E. Troutt III, who had written to inquire what he needed to do to be more useful. Deloria, in very frank language, said that Troutt and other white academics needed to stop feeling "guilty" and needed to stop "trying to help the Indians."

Deloria then laid out in very clear terms what would actually be required for Natives and anthropologists to have an improved relationship. "What is really needed by Indians," he said,

> is anthros who can help us search out certain writings, papers, studies and theories which we can already detect would have a certain value to us but which we had not the foggiest idea of where to look for them. If we had some means of describing a certain situation—i.e., the role of religion in a differentiated and undifferentiated society and the respective functions in each political action, we would be able to use these materials to orient our tribal leaders and others into the theoretical alternatives which they might have that they have not considered.[19]

In closing, Deloria bluntly declared,

Indians hate white anthros because they are always trying to be Indians and they lord their secret knowledge
over Indians as if they were possessors of some great
truth. While Indians don't articulate doctrines in the
same way there are a lot of ideas that each group is expressing that could be communicated to society at large
if techniques of *translation and transmission* [emphasis
his] were developed.[20]

He had similar correspondence with Robert Lane, an anthropologist working in the Northwest. Interestingly, Lane was
married to Barbara Lane, also a well-respected anthropologist
who was working at that time directly with several Native nations on their fishing rights. Her expert testimony and research
would later be useful in the reestablishment of the tribal nations'
treaty right to fish in the region through the *Boldt* decision.
What is notable in his letter to Robert Lane is Deloria's candid
explanation of his political strategy and description about his
own identity.

As for strategy, he said,

I do not believe that demonstrations can carry a group
of 1 million in a nation of 203 million very far without
getting them squashed. So in a certain sense we have to
find leverage points and play with meaningless stereotypes to drive wedges into the outside walls which encompass us. The Indian issue, as I see it, is reconstituting
an undifferentiated worldview which can feel comfortable with electronic technology yet find a human social
value system beyond Christian economic Darwinism.[21]

Deloria then said that he and a leading non-Indian historian
who "always tries to compete with me as to who is the greater Indian," had issues that left them both wanting from an Indigenous
perspective. "I am," said Deloria, "really a political-poet with a
contemporary Indian background—a Zionist who does not relate
to the Hebrew-Indian tradition except as a way to keep oppressors
from the real traditionalists."[22]

Not long after this, Deloria confronted his relationship with the Episcopal Church. He had been elected to the Executive Council in 1968, but by the fall of 1969 was already deeply frustrated by the church leadership's lack of progress on Indigenous issues. In September he wrote Reverend G. H. Jack Woodard:

> I will be submitting my resignation … in the next week and going into the hills to join the gathering hostiles and pagans. I realized from the beginning that it was a slight outside chance to get Indians on the agenda of the church, hence when it has now become apparent that few people either on staff or council have the conceptual context to understand the Indian situation, I would feel that it is disruptive to continue to bring Indian concerns and concepts to the attention of the church.[23]

"We shall simply," said Deloria,

> have to go on and do our thing and when the church wakes up we will have passed far beyond them. At any rate I can't see staying in the church and struggling for years to get the church to act while the rest of the Indian world marches on beyond Christianity. Personally I have to maintain my political position with respect to the movements in Indian Affairs and so I must switch early or not at all.[24]

Bringing Activism into the Academy

During the early 1970s he produced a number of important works, including *We Talk, You Listen* (1970), *Of Utmost Good Faith* (1971), *The Red Man in the New World: A Politico-Legal Study with a Pageantry of American Indian History* (1971), *God Is Red* (1973), and *Behind the Trail of Broken Treaties* (1974). These works coincided with his early involvement in the Academy. He accepted teaching engagements at Western Washington University (1970–1972); UCLA (1972–1973); Pacific School of Religion, Berkeley, California (1975); New School of Religion, Pontiac, Michigan (1976); and Colorado College (1977–1978).

In April 1973, Deloria wrote John Hadsell at the San Francisco Theological Seminary to inform Hadsell of his desire to begin work on an advanced degree at the seminary. He introduced himself as an "Indian political activist and writer and not a professional clergyman," but emphasized that he had no intentions of entering the ministry. What he intended was to "continue studies in the philosophical basis of religions and religious experiences and expressions."[25] Deloria described his scholarship, and stressed that his latest book, *God Is Red*, was due out in the fall.

"The reason I would like to undertake studies in theology at this late date," Deloria explained, "is that I would like to develop a theology of nature based upon the American Indian experiences and beliefs which can be used to bridge the gap between peoples and between the current concern for ecology and the traditional Christian doctrines of exploitation of nature." He continued by noting that the recent Wounded Knee crisis in South Dakota, "if placed in the context of the Old Testament prophets concerned with land reform would be a startling ethnological event in itself." "I feel," he concluded, "that a great deal of new material from the American Indian experience would produce some theological insights for the world today that would be quite creative and unexpected. I would like to try and develop this theme."[26]

In 1978, Deloria accepted a tenured position as professor of law and political science at the University of Arizona. It was there he developed the first MA degree in federal Indian policy, under the rubric of political science, which was later transformed to a degree in American Indian studies. This was the program where I began my work with him. He left Tucson in 1990 and was tenured in history, law, religious studies, and political science at the University of Colorado in Boulder. He remained in Boulder until retirement in 2000, although he and his wife split residency, living in Tucson, Arizona, for part of the year.[27]

For Deloria, being an active participant in life was always about dignity and respect, sovereignty and self-determination, sacredness of space and place, interdependency and interrelatedness, and, ultimately, maturity—individual, national, intercultural, and intergovernmental maturity. Arguably the most intellectually gifted and articulate spokesperson for Indigenous nationhood, Deloria was never quite comfortable with the notion that he was, in fact, the principal champion of tribal nations and their citizens, since he demanded that each Native nation and every tribal citizen express confidence in their own distinctive identities, develop their own unique talents, and wield their collective and individual sovereignty in a way that enriched not only their own nations but all those around them.

Deloria fought tirelessly for *human*, not just Indigenous, freedom and for ecological respect and common sense approaches to heal the environment's gaping wounds. He saw that America's national soul would never be cleansed until justice had been fully achieved by Indigenous nations, African Americans, Latin Americans, Asian Americans, women, impoverished whites, other disempowered groups, and especially young people.

He knew that lasting freedom and justice could only be achieved when those wielding political, legal, and economic power acted with decency and integrity and had engaged in a thorough and honest examination of history. Of course, the dispossessed and disadvantaged also had an active role to play. He expected the leaders of those communities to take the time to carefully articulate the needs and goals of their constituencies.

Deloria's voluminous and diverse written works and his constant engagement with various human communities, especially during the last four decades of his life, are undeniable. But understanding the volcanic and nourishing power that animated him is not easy, since his life and his actions reflected a man of unusual talent, fortitude, and insight. Edward Said once described intellectuals as "exiles," since in a metaphysical sense they were always in the state of "restlessness, movement, constantly being unsettled, and unsettling others."[28] And, according to Said, "The *exilic* intellectual does not respond to the logic of the conventional but to the audacity of daring, and to representing change, to moving on, not standing still."[29]

Deloria was never quite comfortable with being identified as an "intellectual," but much of what Said had to say about intellectuals clearly applies to him, especially Said's discussion of the state of "marginality" that many intellectuals find themselves in—a state that exists outside the halls of privilege and power and yet is one that also carries certain recognition. Deloria, in fact, had a remarkable ability to slide back and forth between various poles, as evidenced by these apparent dichotomies.

He exhibited the committed revolutionary spirit of people like Audre Lorde, Malcolm X, and Cesar Chavez. He was also deeply pragmatic and looked to find ways to resolve the sometimes profound intellectual and normative differences without taking extremist positions that tend to cut off conversation and alienate contending parties.

Deloria could also be described as a generalist or universalist. He had a visionary spirit with the rare ability to scan the intellectual, moral, and political horizon in a comprehensive way that surmounted partisan, racial, tribal, and ideological differences. He was also a grounded and stalwart Standing Rock tribal citizen who drew immense strength and knowledge from his deep and particular kinship ties with his extended family and tribal nation.

Deloria was notorious for his incisive critical abilities that he used to skewer outmoded and prejudicial social norms, stodgy academic institutions and disciplines, and inflated political egos—whether tribal, state, or federal. While he could be formidable in his assessments, he rarely fell into cynicism, always believing that if good people acted from good values and time-honored traditions, they and the institutions they represented would make appropriate decisions more often than not.

He always remained fiercely independent—never allowing blind loyalty to particular institutions or power brokers to interfere with his ability and need to pursue and speak truth to power. That said, he accepted the reality that as a tribal person he had a clear moral and intellectual responsibility to help family, friends, nations, and others in need because of the paradigm of interrelatedness and interdependence that he knew were vital to the welfare of the nations, the state, and the planet.

Finally, while Deloria was truly a public figure, with all the attendant duties and energy-sapping obligations that come with that role, he remained an intensely private person, always looking to maintain a comfortable, quiet space for himself and his family.

At his memorial service in 2005, Norbert Hill, one of his closest friends, noted that with his passing "the training wheels have been taken off," and that it was now essential for everyone to continue the struggle that Deloria had brilliantly led for so long, relying instead on our own individual and collective knowledges and talents. It is unquestionably true that we in Indian Country were overly dependent on Deloria's penetrating intellect, biting wit, and astute political, legal, and cultural strategies.

I am convinced that our overdependence on this esteemed warrior contributed to his premature passing. Therefore, as we, along with the ever-present ember of his filterless Pall Malls, bear some culpability we are obliged to continue the central battles that he valiantly fought throughout his life.

The Delorian Trilogy

Every generation seems to produce a small number of truly visionary individuals—those who not only possess the ability to constructively analyze what is both sound and problematic in society, but who also have the rarer gift of being able to propound suggestions, ideas, and prognostications on what might be done to improve the human condition, both individually and collectively.

In the breadth and depth of Deloria's copious works across several disciplines one finds many such societal, structural, and attitudinal critiques, and, more importantly, for purposes of this book, a bounty of suggested reforms, strategies, and policy recommendations that, if implemented, would produce immediate and sustainable improvements for both Indigenous and non-Indigenous communities.

Some of Deloria's key suggestions and concepts have already been incorporated into policy, law, and intergovernmental relations. Perhaps most profound, explained in his seminal polemic

Table 1

Recommendations for Native Peoples and Governments

Date	Source	Recommendations	Responses
1965	Senate committee testimony	Native nations should contribute their political, economic, and social knowledge whenever there is an opportunity to address societal concerns or promote cultural interaction.	Native nations have become involved in all aspects of politics and society. Many tribes have successful economic development projects, and Indigenous peoples are leaders in social justice and environmental protection movements.
1969	*Custer Died for Your Sins*	Governmental reforms grounded in tradition: a. Youth should seek out and establish relationships with reservation-based, traditional people. b. Tribal governments should adopt policies regarding the scope and structure of proposed research projects. c. Researchers should be required to generate funds for tribal budgets that match their own funding. d. Indians should develop a common law comparable to English common law but based in broadly shared Indigenous values. Tribal governments would mediate between nations and the US while internal affairs would operate within a traditional, clan system structure. e. Reservation and urban program administrators should work together to meet the needs of both communities. Migration, both voluntary and forced, between reservations and urban areas has strained kinship ties and impeded sharing of traditional ways. Deloria predicted recolonization of reservation areas when Native peoples would return or reclaim their rightful homelands.	Related actions: a. Youth programs exist but more are needed. b. Some tribal governments have set parameters on outside research projects, as well as those generated by Native studies programs linked to reservations. c. Academics, often focused on budgetary concerns, do not systematically share funding or findings with Native communities. Native academics, building careers within inherently racist institutions, often produce work that is neither useful to nor understood by their own peoples. d. No significant action. e. Work has been done to maintain connections between reservation and urban Indians, but Native populations in cities such as Denver, Minneapolis, and Seattle remain disconnected from homelands and cultures.
1971	*Of Utmost Good Faith*	American Indians should craft a broad "philosophy of Indian affairs as well as arrive at an understanding of tribalism."	No substantive action.
1972	*The Indian Historian*	Institutional reforms a. A convention should unite national organizations in an effort to create a pan-Indian national organization. Entities such as AIM, NCAI, NIYC, and NTCA would create multilateral positions and a platform for shared purpose.	Accompanying actions to date a. No substantive overarching efforts. b. No substantive action taken. c. This situation has changed and improved with technology and social media access.

		b. Concentrate Indian education programs into fewer locations with more support instead of spreading resources thinly across many institutions. c. Indians must be more judicious in how they work with mass media to avoid exploitation and reinforcement of negative stereotypes. d. Academic conferences should be consolidated. e. Indian tribes should hire full-time lobbyists and have them in every state capital to improve tribal-state relations.	d. There are fewer major conferences, which likely is due to budgetary challenges and technological advances in communication rather than a concerted effort to consolidate. e. Many tribes have hired their own lobbyists, and some are represented in state legislatures by Indigenous state lawmakers.
1973	"The Indian World Today"	Deloria argued that protests should not completely follow the model of Black militants and that Indian activists needed to pinpoint precisely the background of their own oppression. He further argued that tribal leaders should be chosen on the basis of their willingness to work for the self-determination of their nations and not for their own personal political power.	While there were similarities, Native consciousness became the focus and driver of many activists. While this is the ideal, there are many leaders who remain self-serving.
1974	"The Next Three Years"	Natives need to force the federal government to reconsider laws, rules, and regulations that have long oppressed them.	US has instituted "consultation" protocols that have helped, but consultation is different from "consent."
1974	"Religion and Revolution Among American Indians"	Tribal religions must create new forms and ceremonies to confront new conditions. The "tribe" should become identified at its core as a "religious community." Three central areas of future: Higher education, culture, and Native control of educational institutions. Education should address tribal histories and epistemologies, as well as preparation for the larger world. One-year breaks at intervals are needed to allow for cultural and spiritual growth.	Some Native communities are making strides in this arena. No substantive action. Tribally controlled colleges and community colleges are making significant improvements in educational attainment for Native students.
1980	Congressional testimony	Control of Indian education must be returned to local communities and focus on the content and substance of Indigenous traditions. Tribal leadership should be measured by its ability to maintain and adhere to cultural needs and standards that utilize traditional mechanisms.	Indian charter schools and survival schools operate on a number of reservations and in urban communities. Some Native nations have instituted cultural literacy standards that impact policy making.

Table 1 (cont.)

1982	"American Indians: Landmarks on the Trailhead"	There is a need for a national study of Indian voting patterns.	A few political scientists are beginning to track Native voting habits.
1983	*American Indians, American Justice*	Tribal judiciaries and jurists should be careful about the wholesale adoption or mimicking of state or federal structures and procedures in their judicial systems.	Several Native governments, like the Navajo Nation and the Mississippi Choctaw, have created Peacemaker Courts that rely on traditional community leaders and nonadversarial proceedings.
1984	*The Nations Within*	Native nations must structurally reform their governing institutions. They must also reconcile their cultural identity in contemporary America. Native governments must become more economically stable and encourage more amicable relations with state governments, where possible.	A number of nations are engaged in efforts to improve governance and strengthen democratization. Gaming revenues are helping many tribal governments buy and/ or consolidate lands, enrich their cultural identity, and improve relations with the states and local governments.
1985	"Out of Chaos"	Natives must develop a new interpretation of their religious traditions with a universal application.	Progress varies across Indian Country.
1994	*Indian Education in America* ✓	Native students must gain an understanding of their own knowledge systems, and Native academics should work with their communities to create scenarios to resolve pressing community problems. Every Native youth should be taught family genealogy.	Progress varies across Indian Country.
1995	"Rethinking Tribal Sovereignty"	Tribal nations can only claim they wield internal sovereignty if they revive and practice social and cultural traditions to address contemporary issues.	Progress varies across Indian Country.
2001	*We, the People*	Native governments must establish research institutions to meet their many needs. They should revitalize kinship patterns and clan systems to strengthen and legitimize cultural sovereignty.	Progress varies across Indian Country.
2003	*Native Voices*	Urged Natives to deconstruct the principle of consent and move away from consultation.	No substantive action.
2006	*The World We Used to Live In*	Called for Natives to pay more attention to traditional ceremonies.	Native communities are increasingly committed to revival of these traditions.
2009	*C. G. Jung and the Sioux Traditions*	Encouraged Natives to adopt a more comprehensive understanding of the "Seven Generations" construct.	The concept remains widely misused, fostering a dehumanizing myth of Natives as naive visionaries. Use of this simplistic trope, while seemingly inspirational, degrades Native peoples, as the preternatural powers it invokes obscure the true logic, intelligence, and dedication to kinship of their forbears.

Table 2

Recommendations for Federal and State Governments

Date	Source	Recommendations	Responses
1965	Senate committee testimony	Train federal judges in judicial procedures and Native treaty history.	Organizations such as the National American Indian Court Judges Association provide training and guidance. A few university-based programs now exist.
1969	*Custer Died for Your Sins*	US Congressional action ideas: a. Recognize tribes' inherent sovereignty through official policy. b. Restore land to tribes through legislation. c. Recognize status and rights of Eastern tribes with a "blanket law." d. Initiate a "general policy of restitution." e. Promote self-sufficient development of human and natural resources. f. Instigate fundamental reforms within the Bureau of Indian Affairs (BIA).	Related actions to date: a. No substantive response. b. No substantive response. c. No substantive response. d. Land claims were started but not to the extent recommended. e. Indian Self-Determination Act and Education Assistance Act. f. Some reforms undertaken.
1970	*We Talk, You Listen*	Self-determination and sovereignty should be respected.	No substantive response.
		Federal government should develop a national land-use policy.	No substantive response.
1971	*Of Utmost Good Faith*	Federal plenary power must be constrained.	No substantive response.
		The US must resolve legal and moral liabilities for all Indian massacres.	Sand Creek Massacre site received historic landmark designation.
1972	"The BIA, My Brother's Keeper"	Role of the US secretary of the interior must be reformed.	No substantive response.
		Binding arbitration should replace adversarial litigation to resolve disputes.	No substantive response.
1973	*God Is Red*	Reconciliation must occur between Native nations and the US.	No substantive overarching efforts.
1973	*Akwesasne Notes* ✓	Create block grants with money currently spent on simply studying Indians.	Amendments to the Indian Self-Determination and Education Assistance Act and Indian Self-Governance Act created some grant programs.
1974	*Behind the Trail of Broken Treaties*	Domestic and international recognition of Indigenous nationhood.	Some progress with the UN Declaration on the Rights of Indigenous Peoples.
		Initiate a new round of treaties.	No substantive response.

Table 2 (cont.)

1974	*The Indian Historian*	The US must clarify policies, streamline programs, and deal honestly with all Indian communities.	Some progress but no substantive overarching efforts.
1974	*The Indian Affair*	Concentrate attention on treaties.	No substantive response.
		Congress must require checks and balances in Indian affairs.	No substantive response.
1975	*Akwesasne Notes*	Clarify Indian legal, political, and territorial status.	No substantive response.
1976	"The Twentieth Century"	Establish a federal commission to resolve the Black Hills land issue.	No substantive response.
1976	"The Western Shoshone"	Congress should fully investigate actions of the Indian Claims Commission.	No substantive response.
1977	*A Better Day for Indians*	Tribes and the US should work together to a. Set criteria for uniform recognition of Indian communities. b. Clarify definition of tribal citizenship. c. Identify a standard definition of status of Indian tribes. d. Create a "Court of Indian Affairs." e. Undertake arbitration for long-standing claims. f. Rejuvenate the Indian land base. g. Determine a clear universal eligibility for government aid.	Related actions to date: a. BIA established seven criteria in 1978—problems continued. b. No substantive response. c. No substantive response. d. No substantive response. e. Some claims resolved. f. Limited action—enactment of the Indian Land Consolidation Act. g. No substantive response.
1983	*American Indians, American Justice*	Resolve the structural and ethical dilemma with the Solicitor's Office and the Department of Interior.	No substantive action.
		Reduce secretary of the interior's power over tribes.	Congress modified this power in 1968. However, the secretary of the interior's power was not limited until passage of the Indian Tribal Economic Development and Contract Encouragement Act.
1983	Conference presentation	Overturn the doctrine of plenary power.	No substantive action.
1984	*The Nations Within*	Stabilize political relationships between federal, state, and tribal governments to provide a foundation for tribal economic development.	Some improvements have been seen, including retrocession of powers ceded under PL280 by some tribes and development of cross-jurisdictional partnerships at the state and local levels.
		Fully recognize Indian land ownership.	No substantive action.
		Respect and restart the treaty process.	No substantive action.
		Utilize arbitration and mediation to resolve disputes.	Some efforts to avoid costly litigation.

1984	*The Aggressions of Civilization: Federal Indian Policy Since the 1880s*	Restore the bilateral trust relationship that was severely diluted by the Indian Delegation Act of 1946.	No substantive action.
1987	Congressional testimony	US Congressional actions needed: Clarify that legislation is inapplicable to tribes unless explicitly included.	No substantive action.
		Declare that any program to be instituted in Indian Country must first have the consent of affected tribal citizens.	No substantive action.
		Express that treaties establish a unique legal and moral relationship between tribal nations and the US.	No substantive action.
		Hearings on the Indian Claims Commission and problems arising from AIRFA.	No substantive action.
1999	*Tribes, Treaties, and Constitutional Tribulations*	The process of negotiating diplomatic accords, also known as treaties, should be restarted.	No substantive response.
2000	Interview	Tribes, Congress, and the courts should work to rectify the denial and suppression of accurate aboriginal history.	No substantive action at these levels; however, some states are implementing mandatory inclusion of tribal histories in their K–12 curricula.
2001 ✓	"Vine Deloria"	Native nations must cooperate in the creation of a comprehensive plan that details the economic, cultural, and political effects of various disastrous federal policies on their nations.	No substantive action.
2011	*The Legal Universe*	US should revive and incorporate Locke's broader definition of property.	No substantive action.

Custer Died for Your Sins (1969), was the concept of Indigenous sovereignty, which he articulated in a way that made sense for Native peoples politically, legally, and, most importantly, culturally. He believed that cultural integrity was the heart of Native sovereignty, with that integrity having been fully acknowledged in the several hundred treaties that had been signed and ratified by the United States. "Congressional policy," he noted, "should recognize the basic right to tribal sovereignty. Such sovereignty should include all promises contained in treaties and should recognize the eligibility of tribal governments for all federal programs which are opened to counties and cities.... Tribes would be free to develop or not, according to the desires of the people in the tribe."[30] *Sovereignty* is a word so ubiquitous and misused that we forget its origins and fail to appreciate its true meaning. Deloria was very deliberate in his definition, and it was from this point that the term gained its true power and came to be widely understood.

Second, and fundamentally related to Indigenous sovereignty, was the conceptualization of the essential doctrine of tribal self-determination, which debunked and replaced the legally and morally reprehensible federal policy of "termination." The concept of self-determination was formally codified in federal law in another Deloria recommendation—that as self-determined peoples Native nations had the right to subcontract specific services from the Bureau of Indian Affairs (BIA) under Public Law 93-638, the Indian Self-Determination and Education Assistance Act of 1975.[31]

The third and final example is acknowledgment and recognition of the sacred. Prior to the publication of *God Is Red* (1973), there was virtually no discussion in academic or national political halls about the importance and sacredness of space and place for Indigenous nations. This concept is now so ingrained that the word *sacred* within the context of Indigenous peoples' rights and culture is a familiar one even for the broader society. The Water Protectors at Standing Rock in support of the Missouri River and the Lummi Nation in their defense of Cherry Point against fossil fuel exporters used it to explain their actions to the media and before the courts. Defending sacred places is viewed as a just and worthy cause.

Deloria, in reflecting on his work, and in particular, his research and thoughts on these three ideas, noted that "these concepts form the major framework of the federal relationship with Indian tribes."[32] This is certainly the case, and much of the fortunes of Native nations today are derived from their ability to effectively conceptualize and fundamentally implement their national sovereignty, their inherent right of self-determination, and retain and enhance their relationship with the remains of their sacred territory.

As this Delorian trilogy of essential doctrines has provided a paradigm for the resurgence of Indigenous nationhood, it makes intuitive and practical sense to consider other concepts and recommendations he provided that might also prove important to furthering and solidifying the inherent rights of Native nations. These ideas, it will be argued, can provide federal-level political and legal branches with ideas on how to improve their relationships to these nations, and also provide moral and strategic guidance for the Nations themselves.

On Maturity and Interdependence

In the latter stages of his public life, Deloria produced a number of impressive studies—*The Aggressions of Civilization* (coedited with Sandra Cadwalader in 1984), *The Nations Within* (coauthored with Clifford M. Lytle in 1984), *Red Earth, White Lies* (1987), *Tribes, Treaties, and Constitutional Tribulations* (coauthored with David E. Wilkins in 1999), *Power and Place* (coauthored with Daniel Wildcat in 2001), *Evolution, Creationism, and Other Modern Myths* (2002), and *The Legal Universe* (coauthored with David E. Wilkins, 2011)—all incisive critiques of federal Indian policy, constitutional law, education, and scientific knowledge.

Deloria also wrote a set of thematically connected works that thoroughly explored the rich world of religion, spirituality, metaphysic, and philosophy. These studies include *God Is Red* (1973), *The Metaphysics of Modern Existence* (1979), *For This Land* (1998), *Spirit and Reason* (1999), *The World We Used to Live In* (2006), and *C. G. Jung and the Sioux Traditions* (2009).

Although *God Is Red*, the comparative analysis of Native and Judeo-Christian religious traditions, appeared six years before *The Metaphysics of Modern Existence* and was Deloria's second most popular book after *Custer*, it was in *Metaphysics* where one can find the most detailed exploration and articulation of a new metaphysical framework. Here, Deloria sought to synthesize the critical insights of Native peoples—their values, spiritual traditions, ecological practices, and social organization—with those of contemporary Western scientists, philosophers, and theorists who were seeking to understand and arrive at a new vision for the future that accurately and appropriately dealt with reality.

While the core trifecta of sovereignty, self-determination, and space and place continued to have significant meaning, in *Metaphysics* Deloria discussed, challenged, critiqued, and synthesized on a much grander scale—a planetary scale. In this important study he added to his earlier trilogy of concepts additional terms: *interdependence* or *interrelatedness* and *maturity.*

The idea of interdependence or interrelatedness was two-tiered. It was based on the notion that there was a need to transcend the traditional Western monopoly on human knowledge by broadening and linking new knowledge to that of non-Western knowledges—particularly that held by Indigenous peoples. The concept also comported with the fundamental Indigenous idea that all species and all beings are organically and morally related to one another, and that we have an emotional and kinship obligation to treat all beings with respect.

Moreover, Deloria was convinced that a synthesis of what we *believe*—science and religion— and how we *act*—politics, property, ecology, and social relations—is vital, not simply for improved intercultural, interracial, and interspecies relations, but for the very survival of the planet. He contended a synthesis of our beliefs and actions—all essential human experience—needed to fit together in a comprehensive and comprehensible unity if we were to survive the exponential changes driven by increasingly sophisticated technologies that promised to alter every aspect of our existence—communications, economics, science, religion, the environment, politics, and even our traditional cultural norms.

It is interesting that Deloria anticipated the profound power of these technological catalysts before anyone had used a cell phone, sent an email, organized via social media, or had any inkling of the consequences of cyberattacks on international events outside of an episode of *Star Trek.*

Although he could clearly see that ever-more sophisticated technologies would become ubiquitous, Deloria sometimes stubbornly resisted use of communication devices. He held the use of

PowerPoint in particular disdain, viewing it as a crutch that allowed the user to focus on the tool, rather than taking the time to hone the speaking and listening skills necessary to sustain oral traditions. While there was merit in this point of view, his bias against such tools, including video recording, meant that knowledge he worked so tirelessly to gather and share was sometimes lost.

This occurred in the late 1990s, when he organized an extraordinary set of conferences on traditional knowledge. The gatherings were held in different locations throughout Indian Country, and many elders, most of whom have since walked on, came to share sacred memories and knowledge. Deloria had the hope and expectation that the information would be remembered and passed on orally as it had always been; therefore, he allowed no recording devices. Unfortunately, many attendees who received the knowledge, having been trained to rely on modern technologies, did not have the skills to either recall or share what they heard, so the content of these gatherings—even written evidence of their occurrence—has been lost. I believe Deloria would have come to an uneasy compromise with technology and found ways to use it that would have comported with his philosophy, but he did not live long enough to find this balance.

The second major concept that emerged in *Metaphysics* was his notion of maturity. As he put it, there has occurred for Western polities

> a centuries-long process of fundamental change in which the triumphant Western world view of colonial days is replaced by a planetary understanding of the meaning of human existence that so transcends particular national differences as to enable the human species to create a planetary space in the absence of an imperial power to enforce its particular institutions on anyone. In short, a coming to maturity of the human species.[33]

Here, again, years before the concept of globalization became part of our shared worldview, is evinced Deloria's ability to envision the logical trajectory of human experience. It is interesting to me that, in spite of his often-expressed mistrust in technology and misgivings about humankind, Deloria ultimately believed such maturity was possible.

These terms, *interdependence/interrelatedness* and *maturity*, would reappear in many of Vine's later works dealing with religion, philosophy, theology, and history, as he constantly searched to find the most relevant and accessible language that would allow him to reach across cultural, ethnic, political, and legal boundaries. In one interview he observed that "differences in people are not usually evolutionary differences but are differences of metaphysical viewpoint, of ways of looking at, understanding, and interpreting the events and experiences of the world."[34]

In 1979, Deloria appeared cautiously optimistic that the bolder, more risk-taking Western thinkers in the social and physical sciences, and even some religious writers, were on the cusp of arriving at entirely new interpretations of much of the phenomena they studied. He felt it might finally be possible that these brave theorists were offering objective, tangible proof in support of non-Western and Indigenous understandings regarding historical developments, the life of our planet, and even the universe itself. Such a synthesis, an articulation of a new metaphysics, would be of real benefit—not only to Indigenous peoples who for too long had been ignored or derided, but all other peoples as well. Deloria knew that such a radical reorientation of reality would not be accomplished without enormous intellectual conflict, but he was anxious to fully engage all the parties and was prepared to consider all points of view as part of this essential process.

A Natural Responsibility

Now, more than a decade after his passing, we see many examples of Western-centric scholarship's affirmation of traditional knowledge. While it was widely and erroneously believed that Native peoples came to the Americas over a Bering Sea ice bridge, Deloria scoffed at the idea because he understood that no such story was told by any Native people when they spoke of their origins. Further, linguistic diversity and sophistication, magnitude of cultural differences, increasingly ancient dated evidence, and vast geographical realities rendered such a simplistic story laughable—yet another example of Western colonialism whereby the colonizer seeks to discredit even the origin stories of entire nations through shoddy science.

The other crucial perspective that continues to evolve—especially for those in the West, but also for Indigenous peoples who are continuing their efforts to recover their own deep understanding of their once intimate relationship with the natural world—is that of our responsibility and relationship to the natural world. The Rights of Nature movement, championed so eloquently by Christopher Stone in his seminal work in 1972, *Should Trees Have Standing?*,[35] sought to utilize the legal concept of rights as a means to accord a measure of respect for the inherent autonomy of rivers, trees, animals, plants, and the earth itself.

Two European countries (Switzerland and Germany), two Latin American countries (Ecuador and Bolivia), New Zealand, more than thirty-six US cities, and now at least one Native nation (the Ho-Chunk of Wisconsin), have modified their organic charters in various ways to recognize that the natural world and the great diversity of elements constituting the earth do indeed have the inherent right to exist on their own and to be respected as autonomous entities. Such formal acknowledgments build upon the informal manner in which Indigenous peoples around the world have long understood their organic connection to the lands, waters, and animal and plant species.

An unrelenting advocate for Indigenous knowledges, traditions, values, and principles, Deloria nonetheless knew that Native peoples could not simply return to the manner in which they had historically lived and pull those knowledges, institutions, and values forward into a new century. Nor could the larger society or state look to "borrow" from Native cultures. "We face," he said, "the future immediately, and while we can be aware of the sound basis for primitive beliefs and customs, we can never return to them or take them up, expecting them to save us."[36]

It was more realistic, he pointed out, that "the most fruitful avenues of development today are directing us toward a new type of social existence that parallels primitive peoples', perhaps incorporates some of their insights or unconsciously adopts some of their techniques, but which will be fully modern and capable of providing a meaningful existence." He went on to suggest that

> the importance of these movements for primitive peoples is that as modern industrial society becomes aware of new ways of structuring its understanding of the world, economic and political decisions will begin to reflect a more comprehensive and intelligent view of the world and of our species, thereby taking the pressure, in a political and economic sense, away from the surviving primitive and tribal peoples.[37]

As Native peoples and their allies continue to stand in defense of the earth, water, and all life at a time when many in the broader society see these merely as commodities, Deloria's words take on an even more powerful meaning. In North Dakota, when an oil pipeline pathway was rerouted away from a city occupied and controlled mainly by white people because of the risk of a spill and then sent toward reservation lands, the world watched as the Standing Rock people stood up declaring, "Water is life." The political and cultural coalitions they built continue as others begin to realize their interconnectedness to one another and to the earth. It is fitting that Deloria's home became the epicenter for the practice and dissemination of a new, comprehensive worldview. While the Trump administration first signaled in 2017 its intent to return to more extractive and despoiling ecological practices, forces arrayed against such policies are prepared to continue the struggle that Deloria long advocated.

Visions Tempered by Pragmatism

In my reading of a majority of Deloria's published works, supplemented by various recorded presentations, testimonials, and personal correspondence, I have identified and will discuss a broad cross section of his major policy, structural, and attitudinal recommendations. Given that Deloria was actively involved in politics, activism, and the Academy for four decades, and given the tremendous breadth of his ever-expanding knowledge, trying to sort out how to arrange his suggested reforms was no small feat. While he stated in 1993 that his approach to scholarship had been "ad hoc" and that he had produced "'spur-of-the-moment' political tracts," he also noted a more telling truth—that if one read his scholarship in the context of his life, it was possible to "see a persistent effort to lay down certain kinds of strategies for political action which are consistent form start to finish ... [and] they would be alerted that it is in the actions of my life that theories and ideologies and theologies are worked out."[38]

Deloria went on to discount the quality of his own writing, claiming that it was inconsistent form work to work because, as he put it, "a politician can change his mind, a theologian or a philosopher cannot." But the many readers significantly influenced by his work find little that is weak, harried, or inconsistent about his writing, understanding that his works had different ideological and practical thrusts at different times. There is a dynamism, originality, and elegance to be found within both his prose and scholarship. And following the arc of his work, one senses his keen awareness of the politics and culture of Indian Country and their context within the larger society. With this work, we closely examine his prognostications and admonitions on what could and ought to be done to protect what is important and to correct what ails Indigenous and non-Indigenous America.

The remainder of this book is divided into several chapters, with each following a chronological format from pre-*Custer* to his final works produced posthumously. Chapter 2 details suggested policy and governmental reforms Deloria laid out for the federal (and state) government and its sundry branches and agencies. Chapter 3 contains ideas and reforms he suggested for Native nations and their citizens, as Deloria, unlike many Native activists and academics, never shied away from challenging and admonishing Native nations and their citizens when so moved. Chapter 4 is a brief conclusion that considers future possibilities.

Chapter 2

Paths of Resistance

Challenges, Ideas, and Admonitions to Federal (and State) Governments

During his time as executive director of the National Congress of American Indians (1964–1967), Deloria was active not only in Native affairs but also in work that intended to address broader issues of social and economic injustice for numerous minority groups. For example, in 1965 he was appointed to the board of directors for the Citizens Crusade Against Poverty, along with television celebrity Steve Allen; Martin Luther King Jr.; Dave Sullivan, chief of the Building Service Employees Union; and other prominent civil rights officials and clergymen. Called a "conscience" organization by one union leader, the group's aim was to bring federal aid to the more than 35 million low- to middle-income people in the United States.[39]

He also testified before Congress on a variety of bills that had the potential to impact Indian Country. One such occasion was a 1965 hearing before the Senate Subcommittee on Constitutional Rights of the Committee on the Judiciary. The body was taking testimony on a bill that would eventually become the landmark Indian Civil Rights Act of 1968.[40]

In his remarks, Deloria called upon Congress to provide sufficient funding for Native nations in two distinct areas. He asked for support for the training of Indian trial judges "so that they could understand judicial procedure so that we could begin to build a judicial system with a correct balance of law and custom."[41] This testimony and suggestion was a forerunner to the establishment in 1969 of the National American Indian Court Judges Association, which continues to provide just this kind of training, while relying in part on federal funding.

During the next fifty years, other important congressional actions would follow. In 1993, the Indian Tribal Justice Act assisted in the development of tribal judicial systems.[42] And in 2000 came the Indian Tribal Justice Technical and Legal Assistance Act,[43] which provided technical and legal assistance to tribal justice systems because "enhancing tribal court systems and improving access to those systems serves the dual Federal goals of tribal political self-determination and economic self-sufficiency."[44]

These laws culminated in Congress's 2010 enactment of the Tribal Law and Order Act, which was designed to address crime in Indian Country by emphasizing the critical need to reduce the horrific levels of sexual violence against Native women. The act provided funding to hire more law enforcement officers and restored to tribal courts some authority to prosecute and then mete out punishment to non-Indians who commit the vast majority of crimes against Native women. Such a restoration would not have taken place had Native judicial systems not made such great strides.[45]

When *Custer Died for Your Sins* was published in 1969, the timing of the book's release, the strength of Deloria's trenchant observations, and his sardonic prose assured that the work would have real staying power. Subtitled *An Indian Manifesto*, Deloria surgically attacked many of the entrenched myths about Native peoples and castigated what at that time were the larger society's most powerful institutions—higher education (especially the field of anthropology) and churches. He took the federal government to task for ongoing flawed and woefully inadequate policies for tribal nations. The book also contained a number of ideas and advice on what the federal government should do to improve its relationship to Native nations. These were his major recommendations for Congress:

- Codify a policy that would respect the inherent sovereignty and dignity of Indians; a "cultural leave-us-alone agreement, in spirit and in fact."[46]

- Enact legislation "acknowledging the rights of the Indian people as contained in the treaties, particularly to hunting and fishing rights."[47]

- Act to restore land to tribal nations "by transferring land now held by the various governmental departments within reservation boundaries to the tribes involved. Additional land in the public domain can be added to smaller reservations."[48]

- Enact a "blanket law" recognizing the status and rights of eastern Native peoples and their right to organize under the Indian Reorganization Act (IRA). Federal services could then be made available to these long ignored nations on a "contract" basis that would enable them to eventually attain a measure of economic self-sufficiency.[49] (Note: Had Congress acted upon this recommendation at the time, it is likely that the entire federal recognition process, which has become a political debacle, could have been better administered. Instead, Congress acquiesced and allowed the BIA to establish the problematic "criteria" for what constitutes an "Indian tribe" in 1978, and the process has since been mired in politics and gaming-inspired economics with no logical ending in sight.[50])

- Initiate a "general policy of restitution" that would go far beyond the limited and adversarial scope of the Indian Claims Commission that began in 1946 and was formally terminated in 1978, with many cases still unresolved. Deloria understood that until "past betrayals" were settled, it would be impossible to build an amicable relationship between Native nations and the United States. (Note: A number of eastern Indian land claims were started, with some Native nations, like those in Maine, securing recognized status and having some of their aboriginal lands returned. But the "general policy of restitution" and reconciliation has still not been fully embraced by the federal government, despite Assistant Secretary of Indian Affairs Kevin Gover's formal "apology" to Native peoples in 2000, the $3.4 billion *Cobell* class action settlement approved by Congress in 2009, and the Obama administration's settlement of lawsuits with some seventeen tribal governments in 2016 for about $492 million. *Cobell* and the settlements in 2016 dealt with federal mismanagement of tribal funds, allotments, and resources, many dating back to the General Allotment Act [also known as the Dawes Act] of 1887.)

- Enact a policy that would "promote the development of human and natural resources on the reservations, [with] programs ... philosophically oriented to total development. There would be a means by which development could be evaluated—that of self-sufficiency."[51] (Note: This call for Indian self-determination would, in fact, become law with the enactment of the Indian Self-Determination and Education Assistance Act in 1975.[52])

- Issue a policy that would recognize in every state "the basic right to tribal sovereignty." This "should include all promises contained in treaties and should recognize the eligibility of tribal governments for all federal programs which are opened to counties and cities."[53] (Note: The first part of this statement has not fully been acted upon, but beginning in the 1970s, tribal governments became eligible for what amounted to block grants as governments and not solely because of their tribal status. They have also, more recently, been accorded "treatment-as-state" status so that they can competitively apply for funds in a manner comparable to that of states, especially in the environmental area.)

Deloria had advice for the BIA as well, identifying fundamental changes needed in order for the agency to be more effective. Specifically, he called for the following:

- "Programming by Size of Tribe"—This recommendation was a recognition that, while some larger Native nations were capable of handling large programs, many smaller Indigenous communities with inadequate funding would still need some direct linkage to the BIA.

- "Discretionary Funds"—Another approach that acknowledged the diversity and complexity of tribes called for greater flexibility in the allocation of federal expenditures by the BIA and Native nations. Deloria emphasized that decisions should be made according to Native need and not Washington priorities. (Note: This recommendation was partially fulfilled with the passage in 1988 of the Indian Self-Governance Act, which provided just what Deloria had called for— "maximum flexibility in meeting local needs.")

- "Tribal Employment Would Be Civil Service"—As tribal governments assumed greater control over their own programs and dollars, and with more people leaving the federal work force to be employed by their nations, their Civil Service Status would remain in effect. Thus, "the most capable people would soon be hired for tribal programs."[54]

- "Reorganization of the Bureau of Indian Affairs"—Deloria recommended that the BIA be transferred to the Commerce Department, since economic development, granting, and technical assistance would be the primary functions with the arrival of tribal self-determination.

    Science for Tribes

- "Disposition of Federal Responsibility to Indians"— Native nations would remain eligible for grants from all federal agencies and income generated from tribal lands, and the lands themselves would remain tax exempt "as long as the lands and the income derived from them were used to provide social and community services to reservation residents."[55]

- Contracting with Tribes—Finally, and most directly, Deloria insisted that "the most useful thing Interior and its component bureaus could do in the immediate future would be to begin contracting with tribes and Indian centers to provide a comprehensive national program for development and training."[56] (Note: As stated earlier, when Congress enacted the 1975 Indian Self-Determination Act, the BIA was charged with doing this very thing—subcontracting with Native governments. Although this process and the 1988 Indian Self-Governance Act lacked the comprehensive scope Deloria called for, these were steps in that direction.)

In his second major book, *We Talk, You Listen* (1970), Deloria made two specific suggestions for reform that bear repeating: one regarding the struggles of all minority groups, the other centered on the environment.

On the question of minorities, he suggested that if the federal government was serious about defusing interracial tensions and in improving the socioeconomic position of the members of these racial and ethnic groups, then the self-determination and sovereignty of each group should be respected. In calling for a preferential policy for all oppressed racial and ethnic groups, he noted that "one aspect of change in this area would be the replacement of non-group members by group members in those programs which minister most intimately to specific groups. This would mean that decisions affecting certain groups would be made by the people of those groups."[57]

Although affirmative action was still in its fledgling years, Deloria was advocating something far more powerful and profound: sovereignty. He said official acknowledgment was required to make it clear that specific racial, ethnic, and gender groups have rights as groups that bear specific recognition and treatment. This is most evident in his application of the concept of sovereignty to these groups and their members. "Perhaps," said Deloria, "many cannot conceive of sovereignty outside of a territory within which they can exercise their own will."[58] He believed, however, that that was a far too limited way in which to understand the term. Thus, he emphasized that the "tactical efforts of minority groups should be based upon the concept of sovereignty. Only in this manner can they hope to affect policies which now block them from full realization of the nature and extent of their problems."[59]

Deloria went on to note that the "natural sovereignty" of these groups was implicitly recognized whenever whites would ask the perennial question, "Who are your leaders?" As he astutely observed, "if the whole community is willing to deal only with the leaders of minority groups, is not this the best indication that they somehow understand the natural sovereignty of the group? That they are willing and find a need to negotiate with the rightful government of the group?"[60]

Regarding the environment, Deloria urged that the United States develop a land use plan for the entire country. "The government," he went on, "should repurchase all marginal farm lands and a substantial number of farms in remote areas. This land should be planted with its original growth, whether forest or grassland sod. The entire upper Midwest plains area of the Dakotas and Montana and upper Wyoming should become open-plains range with title in public hands. Deer, buffalo, and antelope should gradually replace cattle as herd animals."[61]

While the slow depopulation by whites of the nation's heartland continues, there is a movement by some on the political right to undermine or altogether eliminate the public lands system. This comes at a time when extraction industries such as coal, oil, and minerals corporations are fighting to control these lands through abuse of the powers of eminent domain and short-term investments in local economies and politicians. They are fighting to continue devastating the environment for the enrichment of a few. Dangerous, polluting practices such as fracking and oil transportation by pipeline serve to enrich a few investors and to boost local economies in the short term.

In the long term, tribes and other local residents are left to deal with the environmental consequences and loss of sacred places. There is, however, a growing movement of small farmers and ranchers who adhere to more ethical, responsible practices centered on health and long-term stewardship. Their ways are finally catching up with traditional Indigenous understandings of the interactions and sustainability of these ecosystems. Native nations are now actively building alliances with small farmers and ranchers to protect the water, land, and wildlife.

In between *Custer* and *We Talk, You Listen*, Deloria planned for a book that he never wrote: a treatise on federal Indian law. In November 1969 he wrote his friend Jack Greenberg of the NAACP Legal Defense Fund and laid out his vision. He had decided to apply for a Guggenheim Fellowship, and if he had secured it, his plan was to spend the next year writing the book.

As he explained to Greenberg, the study would "primarily deal with rights of tribes as tribes" and would not deal as such with the rights of individual Indians. Deloria noted that he had already started the outline and had cross-indexed a majority of the state and federal court cases that addressed Native topics. "What I basically need," he wrote, "is a chance to visit obscure tribes and groups and work out contemporary doctrines on the basis of their needs."

Moreover, "certain procedural aspects of federal courts need to be worked out in relation to individual rights as they are simultaneously tribal rights derived from treaties also. This would take conferences with some of the tribes to discover on what basis they currently conceive of their tribal and treaty rights."[62] The first modern casebook on Federal Indian Law was Monroe Price's study, *Law and the American Indian*, which came out in 1973.[63]

Battling the Many-Faced Demon of Plenary Power

Although Deloria concentrated his attention on Native peoples in the United States, early in his career he paid considerable attention to the status of Indigenous peoples in Canada. In fact, while still a law student in February of 1970, he was invited to McGill University in Quebec to give a keynote address at a conference on North American Indian issues. Deloria was well aware of the struggles of First Nations in Canada, particularly the outrage resulting from the infamous White Paper introduced by Canadian prime minister Jean Chrétien in 1969. If the proposal had been carried out, it would have effectively terminated the treaty rights of all First Nations members.

In a letter to Sanford Smith in February 1970, Deloria intoned, "The situation in Canada with respect to its Indian policy ... is potentially the most dangerous and disastrous policy that has ever been advocated by either Canada or the United States. It attempts to unilaterally sever ALL relationships between Canada and its Indian tribes." "Canada," Deloria continued, "does not even recognize the Aboriginal title to lands which means that its Indians have no rights other than what the Canadian government wishes to acknowledge."[64]

A month later, dealing with the same Canadian theme, Deloria wrote William Paddock and proposed a research idea on Native land that focused on Canada. He told Paddock, "You might begin some preliminary research on building a case that could be presented to the Canadian government for recognition of Aboriginal title in an Indian Claims Commission type forum like we have here in the states."[65]

In *Of Utmost Good Faith* (1971), his first edited book, Deloria emphatically declared that until and unless a way was found to constrain the largely unfettered powers of Congress over Native nations, often referred to as congressional plenary power, Indigenous peoples would remain severely disadvantaged: "There must be a drastic limitation on the ability of Congress to change the status of the Indian tribes at its whim and a redefinition of the scope of administration of Indian affairs by the federal government."[66]

Deloria also decried the fact that the United States still had not fairly resolved its legal and moral liabilities for the massacres of Lakota individuals at Wounded Knee in 1890 or for the Cheyenne and Arapaho at Sand Creek in 1894.[67] The devastating Sand Creek event was partially addressed by federal action in 2000 when President Bill Clinton signed into law[68] a bill introduced by the lone Native senator Ben Nighthorse Campbell (Northern

Cheyenne), that established the site of the Sand Creek Massacre as a national historic landmark. The act set aside an area of about 12,480 acres along Sand Creek in Kiowa County, Colorado, as the territory of the historic site. And although Congress has yet to respond directly on behalf of the ancestors of those who were killed at Wounded Knee, beginning in 1986, Birgil Kills Straight, a Lakota, has led what has become an annual pilgrimage in honor of those massacred by federal forces.[69]

In January 1971, Deloria responded to a letter from Dan Smith of Illinois who questioned why Native peoples in Washington State were not being more physically demonstrative in their battles against the state over fishing rights. He pointed out a glaring demographic reality that always leaves Indigenous peoples at a disadvantage—their sheer lack of numbers. "What do you propose," Deloria asked Smith, "that we send 100 Indians marching out to face the combined strength of the state of Washington to get our fishing rights confirmed? They are already shooting us from ambush out here. They don't have the guts to face us while they kill us and we are outnumbered 3,000,000 to 25,000."[70] Deloria then laid out a strategy that he felt was more conducive to legal and political change: "I am advocating being smarter than they are, using the federal courts and Congress to get as many wrongs corrected as possible, and then hoping that somehow a more intelligent type of white will come into power."

In the spring of that same year, Deloria teamed up with Karen Ducheneaux and Kirk Kickingbird to establish the Institute for the Development of Indian Law (IDIL). The organization, said Deloria, would be scholarly and analytical in its approach to Native legal and political problems. "While it could be called 'IDIL' it will not be. But we do not plan to be active or militant in the usually accepted sense. Rather a serious scholarly back-up center."[71]

The institute's principal goals were to (1) publish an Indian law journal, (2) produce special reports like those provided by the NAACP's Indian education report, (3) conduct seminars for urban center boards and tribal councils on Indian law, (4) disseminate a slip-sheet publication on current legal events, (5) conduct selected research on philosophical topics in Indian law, and (6) engage in selected litigation, primarily intervention into existing lawsuits, submission of amicus curiae briefs, and appeals cases.[72]

Sovereignty Resurrected

Deloria's typewriter, and later his computer, was never at rest for very long, and the 1970s was an exceptionally prolific decade for him as a writer. He produced eight books that encompassed a variety of disciplines, including *God Is Red* (1973), *Behind the Trail of Broken Treaties* (1974), *The Indian Affair* (1974), *Indians of the Pacific Northwest* (1977), and *The Metaphysics of Modern Existence* (1979). Additionally, he authored at least ninety essays, articles, newspaper columns, and other small pieces that dealt with federal Indian policy, religion and theology, social commentary, legal analysis, tribal case studies, education, and social movements. Therein were some of his more trenchant suggestions and recommendations on how the United States could fundamentally improve its relationships with Indigenous nations.

In a 1972 article on the BIA, Deloria acknowledged one of the major and perpetual problems Native nations face in dealing with the federal bureaucracy: "Today, whenever the Bureau doesn't want to do something, it blithely tells Indians, 'the Secretary doesn't have the power to do that.' When it wants to do something it mentions the Secretary's 'inherent' power to act."[73] This fundamental policy inconsistency in the very agency charged most intimately with carrying out the nation's treaty and trust obligations has had severe consequences for Native governments. Deloria suggested as an alternative that "if everyday interpretations could be examined in a non-adversary hearing before a court empowered to arbitrate issues, the Bureau would soon lose its magical power over Indian lives."[74] The idea of binding arbitration, rather than adversarial litigation, continues to hold great promise, particularly given the volatile political nature of Native nations/US relations.

In the early spring of 1972, Deloria received a letter from Jeanette Smith of the Democratic National Committee asking his opinion of the effectiveness of Richard Nixon's 1970 speech on

Indian affairs in which he addressed the concept of Indian self-determination. Deloria, in typically blunt language, said, "I would like to be frank with you. As I have observed, and as I personally feel, the Democrats have lost a lot of ground with the American Indian community in the past four years. Although I am a registered Democrat I will probably support Richard Nixon this fall. I would assume that a great many other Indians will do so also."[75]

He then carefully described seven specific reasons why he and other Natives were likely to support Republicans rather than Democrats in the fall elections. They ranged from the feeling that Democrats "have always taken the Indian vote for granted," to the fact that under the Nixon administration Natives had far greater access to key staff members of the White House, something they did not have during the Kennedy or Johnson administrations. He also pointed out that important Democrats on the Interior Committee opposed the return of Blue Lake to the Taos Pueblo people and that this had had a "very adverse effect on the image of the Democratic party as a liberal or sympathetic party."[76]

Deloria concluded by highlighting the main problem Democrats were having in securing Native support—that while Democratic leaders were all for civil rights, they failed to show support with equal enthusiasm for Native treaty rights. "This," Deloria said, "makes Indians fearful of integration of Indian communities into white society. It loses a lot of votes. The Republicans, of course, have opposed integration and therefore have appealed to Indians quite a bit."[77]

In August 1972, Deloria wrote a detailed letter to Ralph Nader of the Center for the Study of Responsive Law. Nader had been asked to write an investigative report on the relationship between the BIA and Native nations; however, he was apparently reluctant to conduct such a study because he believed that Edgar Cahn's 1969 study, *Our Brother's Keeper: The Indian in White America*,[78] had already covered the issue.

Deloria urged Nader to reconsider, as he was convinced that the Cahn report had not adequately addressed the profundity of Indigenous peoples' problems in the United States. He cited as three examples the ongoing fishing rights struggles of Northwest Native peoples, exploitation of Quinault timber, and the BIA's inability or unwillingness to exercise its treaty and trust responsibilities to assist Native peoples.

"I have also discovered," said Deloria, "a number of other incidents where there appears to be something of an irregular nature happening in Indian affairs…. I would urge," he continued, "that a study quietly be undertaken to investigate the whole complex of relationships that surrounds the Interior Department and affects the decisions affecting Indians that it makes."[79]

In *God Is Red*, Deloria comprehensively noted that "before any final solution to American history can occur a reconciliation must be effected between the spiritual owner of the land—the American Indian—and the political owner of the land—the American white man. Guilt and accusations cannot continue to revolve in a vacuum without some effort at solution."[80] Reconciliation was carried out in South Africa in the wake of apartheid. It has also been attempted in Canada. But it still has never been a process employed in the United States, despite this nation's inglorious history regarding Native peoples, as well as African Americans, beginning with slavery.

Wounded Knees, Wounded Souls

In 1973, *Akwesasne Notes*, then the leading Native news journal, republished an interview Deloria had done with Peter Collier that had first appeared in *Mademoiselle*.[81] Deloria restated two key points—one political, one economic—that still hold relevance. Politically, he said the real crisis in the relationship between Indigenous nations and the United States lay in the fact that the federal government had not yet formally and emphatically recognized that "Indian tribes are sovereign nations as guaranteed in the hundreds of treaties … and that you [federal government] can't interfere with our property rights, life style, anything that is important to us."

Then, from an economic perspective, he reiterated that the federal government should take the sizable amounts of money being spent on "studying Indians [and] having conferences," and place those funds into a large "grant fund and given outright to the small tribes so they can get going." Larger Native governments, like the Navajo Nation, would have a revolving loan fund established so that they would have monies available to them.[82] The block grant idea he proposed would eventually come to pass when Congress amended the Indian Self-Determination and Education Assistance Act in 1988 to provide funds directly to a number of Native governments meeting the criteria.[83] This law was expanded in 1994 in an act popularly known as the Indian Self-Governance Act, and continues to be well received by those nations who participate in the bilateral arrangements.[84]

In April 1973, Deloria wrote an op-ed for the *Los Angeles Times* titled "Bury Our Hopes at Wounded Knee: An Indian's Reflections."[85] He explained the conditions that had fueled the takeover, led by a coalition made up of three disparate groups: the desperate, traditionally minded people who insisted on the vitality of the treaties their ancestors had signed and that the United States only sometimes adhered to; the inspired, and sometimes confused, Native activists; and tribal governments that did important work, yet had long been denied legitimate governing authority. Complicating the situation for some tribal governments was the fear of violent and corrupt individuals such as Richard Wilson, the chairman at Pine Ridge Reservation, home of the Wounded Knee site.

Deloria also complained that, rather than take the time to meet and speak with Native peoples about their issues and concerns, the larger society turned to television personalities like Dick Cavett, celebrities like Jane Fonda, and white academics and literary figures who purported to be experts on tribal matters.

So how does a modern American Indian respond to such a crisis as Wounded Knee? If you don't grab a gun and rush to South Dakota, your liberal friends and militant Indian relatives chastise you for not making the scene of the greatest dramatization of Indian problems ever seen. If you offer your assistance to the forces of law and order, you are refused.

"Wounded Knee 1973," Deloria concluded, "shows one thing very clearly: American Indians are prohibited from having a modern identity. We must dress in buckskin when we protest. But then we are told to work through the system and forget the buckskin. The system, public and private, listens only to the men in buckskin because they're _real_ Indians."

In October 1973, Deloria gave an address at the 64th General Convention of the Protestant Episcopal Church in Louisville, Kentucky. In attendance was Vernon Bellecourt (White Earth Anishinaabe), one of the American Indian Movement's (AIM) foundational figures. As I learned from documents secured from the Federal Bureau of Investigation (FBI) through a Freedom of Information Act (FOIA) request, Bellecourt was under governmental surveillance at the time. The FBI agent assigned to shadow him filed a report a month later noting that "subject [Bellecourt] was observed in attendance at a reception apparently given in honor of Vine Deloria, Jr. ... Deloria reportedly is an Indian author with offices located at 847 E. Colfax, Denver, CO, which is the same building occupied by the American Indian Movement chapter. Deloria allegedly is an AIM sympathizer and supporter of AIM activities."[86] The agent writing the report noted that the information about Deloria had been "furnished by CS"—"CS" being the initials of the undercover person who conducted surveillance on Bellecourt.

Fellow activist LaDonna Harris (Comanche) wrote Deloria in the fall of 1973 asking his views on the status of off-reservation Natives. Deloria responded by letter on October 10 and laid out several useful suggestions that would help clarify the rights of Natives who no longer lived on or near Indian Country. He opened by saying that even the treaties themselves contained language that should be construed to support the rights of all tribal members wherever they resided. "There is one treaty with the Stockbridge-Munsee," he said, "which distinguishes between citizen Indians and non-citizen Indians. Outside of that I think that the responsibility extends to all tribal members wherever they are. And since there are no Indians without a tribe of some kind it would seem to me that the off-reservation people have an equal right to federal services."[87]

As proof of the right of off-reservation Natives to receive federal services, Deloria told Harris that not long prior he had completed a study of higher education programs for Indians and found that "in the Portland and Minneapolis area offices nearly half of the present scholarship grants for college go to students living off the reservation.... While some of this is to students whose parents have 'pull' with the tribal council, it may be that they simply don't want to make formal a situation which already exists." Deloria encouraged Harris to have a researcher go through the BIA's records in all its area offices. He felt confident she would find that "while the BIA doesn't say anything about it, a substantial amount of their college scholarship money presently goes to off-reservation people."[88] Deloria went on to say that while the BIA claimed to be the sole entity responsible for deciding which Natives receive federal services, "that is simply not true. The trust responsibility is a federal responsibility, not an agency or departmental responsibility."

Finally, Deloria addressed the status of tribal persons who migrate to major cities and offered a practical solution to meeting their needs. There should be a provision

> that people of a tribe who wish to re-form into a smaller group could be allowed to do so and maintain federal recognition. For example, the Blackfeet have a very large community in Seattle, WA. For the most part they are people who have left the reservation to live permanently in Seattle. Why not allow them to organize an Indian community there and receive federal recognition, then drop their membership in the reservation community rolls upon receiving recognition as a federal group in Seattle?[89]

The solution to this would be tribal membership cards issued to all eligible members that would be protected through encrypted computer programs. With these cards, even heirship lands could be solved "as tribal members could trade interests in land via computer."

In *Behind the Trail of Broken Treaties*, released in 1974, Deloria provided a powerful argument in support of the inherent nationhood of Native nations—a nationhood that deserved not only domestic but also international political and legal recognition. These are the specific suggestions he made to the federal government: He began by stating that the US government should "recognize the international status of the Indian tribes," while at the same time affirming the ongoing existence of a trust relationship with Indian tribes as smaller nations under the protection of the United States.[90] Importantly, the trust relationship would be redefined from what he labeled an "active trust," where the federal government essentially imposes its will on Indian rights and resources whenever and however it chooses, to that of a "passive trust," with Indigenous governments in charge of their own affairs and generally free from federal dominance.[91]

The notion of a passive trust, if ever fully adopted, would result in a fundamental improvement in Native political and economic status in that the federal government, according to Deloria, would surrender its "right to extinguish Indian aboriginal title to land, and would freeze the present Indian lands within the context of national boundaries rather than reservation boundaries. Eliminating the claim of the United States to first-purchase rights of tribal land would mean that no further sales of Indian lands would be possible. The lands of individual Indians would have to be sold to the tribal government under the same legal terms by which the United States government now purchases tribal lands."[92]

Calling Down the Thunder—
Unleashing the Power of Treaties

Two additional recommendations concern ideas that have recurred throughout many of Deloria's writings: Congress should initiate a new round of treaties and/or agreements with tribal nations, and state governments should be reminded that from a constitutional and treaty perspective they have virtually no more authority "to interfere with tribal governments or reservation affairs than they would to interfere with the operations of the Canadian or Mexican governments."[93]

The relationship between Native nations and states continues to be deeply problematic. On January 26, 2017, two Republican North Dakota state representatives introduced House Concurrent Resolution HCR 3017 that, had it been approved, would have effectively eliminated all reservations in the state because "the current Indian reservation system has become flawed and obsolete."[94] There was swift denunciation from Native leaders about the resolution, and within a week it was withdrawn.

In his capacity as a recognized "expert" on the 1868 Fort Laramie Treaty and Lakota political and religious history and culture, Deloria also somehow found time between 1974 and 1977 to serve as an expert witness and appointed counsel in four trials[95] involving AIM's occupation of Wounded Knee in 1973 and its aftermath. The late, dedicated advocate Larry Leventhal, one of the attorneys representing Dennis Banks and Russell Means, two of the most prominent leaders of AIM, enlisted Vine to serve as an expert witness for the AIM leaders.[96] Leventhal and Deloria had a long-standing relationship before and after the trials. During the Wounded Knee litigation, using Deloria's outstanding testimony, Levanthal was able to convince the court to accept the relevancy and legality of the 1868 treaty and the Lakota's understanding of that treaty as key elements in the trial. "He disarms so many opponents," he once said of Leventhal. "He comes across as the bumpkin. Then all of a sudden you're on the canvas, asking, 'Who was that masked man?'"[97] In an interview from 1998, Deloria described Leventhal as one of the top five lawyers in the country on Indian treaty issues. And, he said, "He's the only one who is white."[98]

During cross-examination by US attorney R. D. Hurd at the four-day trial in August 1974, Deloria was asked, "Generally speaking would it be fair to state then that as to the meaning of the treaty and different phrases within the treaty, different Indians interpret them differently depending upon what you're talking about, and whether or not you are a follower of the oral tradition, or whether or not you read it from the standpoint of modern-day legal interpretation?" Deloria, ever the astute comparativist, said,

Well, let me answer by comparing it to the U.S. Constitution. I think there's a general sense the American people have basic rights under the Constitution, although many may not be able to tell you about what article and clause it's in, and I find that to be the general attitude among Sioux Indians of their treaties. Then there are scholars, technicians, and politicians who deal in very precise phrases of the Constitution, and you have to look at that technical discussion in the general context of everybody accept[ing] the Constitution as a valid document, and that's the way I look at the treaty.

Leventhal then asked Deloria, "Do you have an opinion as to how the 1868 treaty is generally understood by the Sioux?" Deloria responded thus:

Well, I think the overwhelming consensus of the Indian interpretation of the treaty, to me, the vast majority have a tendency to take the treaty literally, the literal words, whatever is there, in the belief this is what the United States put on paper and gave to the Chiefs. In my opinion, getting into the proceedings, the treaty is much stronger than the literal interpretation, but I've been unable to present that point of view to the majority of the people. They insist on the literal interpretation.

Leventhal followed up, "The 1868 Sioux treaty has been described earlier as a sacred document by one of the witnesses from the government. Would you agree, Mr. Deloria, that the 1868 Sioux treaty is a sacred document?" Deloria said, "Yes, that's why I've developed the whole concept of treaty interpretation as a religious issue so it would be understood by people the way Indian people understand it."

Deloria's convincing testimony helped establish the relevancy and validity of Native treaties as central legal documents that could be used by Native nations and their legal teams in court cases. When I interviewed Leventhal in 2009, he made a point of noting that Deloria was a "great resource" in part because "he could work and talk at different levels. He could cite the court cases and cite the cases that talked about the cases as well as cite the laws, and laws that overturned those laws, and write law review articles, and be very specific that way. But he could also talk well to the [Native] activists ... and also the academics ... and the general public."[99]

During this time Deloria contributed an article titled "The Next Three Years" to *The Indian Historian*, in which he included another set of solid policy recommendations that bear consideration.

- The BIA should follow its congressional mandate out-lined in the 1921 Snyder Act (which gave the bureau general authorization to provide various services and benefits to Native peoples throughout the United States) and provide services to Natives wherever they live, both reservation based and urban based.

- As part of this mandate, the BIA should work closely with tribal governments "to bring enrollments up to date and issue each Indian a plastic card with a num-ber on it entitling him or her to receive services."

- A survey should be done of "all existing Indian com-munities" that have retained aspects of Indian life and culture, and these groups should be officially "recog-nized" by the US government and helped to organize themselves politically and economically. This policy, unlike the current ad hoc and largely arbitrary fed-eral acknowledgment process, "would finally bring the executive branch within the law, as defined and articulated by the federal courts, and would enable the Congress to view Indian conditions as a national commitment, and not as a commitment to respond to the political pressures that a few large Western tribes can bring."[100]

These three policy suggestions—a BIA that supports every Native citizen, regardless of location; a clearly defined Indigenous population; and a national commitment to recognize all those bonafide nonrecognized Native peoples—would establish a comprehensive federal basis that would, in turn, also encompass the protection of remaining tribal natural resources, federal education policy, and employment and housing for Native communities. The key to these suggestions would be the comprehensiveness of the federal commitment. As Deloria noted in conclusion, "We are at the stage where we must force the government to clarify its policies, to streamline its programs and to deal honestly with all Indian communities, large and small, eastern and western, urban and rural."[101]

The status of nonrecognized Native communities was one that frustrated him, given his belief that the federal trust relationship extended to "all" Native peoples. In a letter to Kent Connally in January 1974, Deloria laid out a powerful theoretical position for nonrecognized Native nations. He said,

> I think that all tribes that are now unrecognized are in an 'aboriginal state' in that while the federal government has not recognized them they have really lost nothing of the political status enjoyed by all tribes of the continent prior to the coming of the white man. Therefore they possess all attributes of a tribe at any time in history when the white man first came. This idea can be pushed to ridiculous extremes by activists and so I don't usually mention it because it simply forms the theoretical basis for beginning to derive an argument for recognition."[102]

Battling Federal Discretionary Powers

In *The Indian Affair*, a short, incisive book written in 1974, Deloria continued his focused assault on all that had gone wrong in Indigenous affairs: from their myriad and unique legal problems, to the need for genuine control of Native education, to a critical discourse on the role the churches and missionaries had played, with a sharp analysis of how Native peoples had struggled to resist church advances on their souls, their rights, and their resources. In a chapter titled simply "The Federal Government," Deloria made three searching points. First, that treaty rights, which are "central to the solution of today's problems," are very complicated and require concentrated and detailed attention. While noting that Natives are not always clear on what their rights and responsibilities are under treaties, Deloria contended that "it is the Congress that must be blamed for the violation of treaties, since it was the Congress that passed the General Allotment Act, developed the termination policy, and has abdicated its responsibility for overseeing Indian programs."[103]

Second, and related to the first, is that since Congress too often abdicates its legislative responsibility, the secretary of the interior is allowed to step in and provide interpretations of laws and regulations that often conflict with Native views of their rights. This becomes a major burden for Native nations because "the only appeal to an administrative ruling is through the administrative processes, so the Interior Department and Bureau of Indian Affairs act as legislator, court and administrators of the laws pertaining to Indians."[104] This structural lack of checks and balances remains one of the major roadblocks to genuine Native self-determination.

Finally, Deloria pointed out that the federal courts constitute yet another major structural and ideological barrier Indigenous peoples face. Although many powerless groups, including Native nations, frequently turn to the federal courts for justice, this tactic has proven extremely problematic for two reasons. Federal judges and justices generally lack the substantive knowledge of Native history and treaty law necessary to render fair and accurate judgments. And, since one of the core doctrines of interpretation in federal Indian law is that "in the absence of a clear statement interpreting a statute or treaty, the courts will look to the administrative practices of the executive branch to determine how to decide a case,"[105] Native rights are left vulnerable to administrative discretionary power. For Native people in a treaty relationship to the United States, this means if the BIA and the federal government have consistently acted to disregard a treaty's provisions for a considerable time, "the court will decide the treaty invalid; if it were valid, then quite obviously the BIA would have respected and followed it."[106] Such a situation leaves tribal nations in virtually winless situations, since the three coequal branches of the federal government, having failed in their treaty and constitutional obligations to Native nations, then blame the other branches for their own failures.

Fractured Legacies

One of the most daunting problems plaguing Native peoples for decades in Indian Country is the status of their lands—both those held by the nations and individual allotments and interests. Within this broad sphere of land issues, it is heirship problems, particularly those caused by fractionated allotments, that predominate. These are especially complex and have proven difficult to resolve by the federal government, which is ironically responsible for having created and exacerbated the problem dating back to the General Allotment Act in 1887.

That disastrous policy, which affected nearly 200 reservations, allotted reservations lands into 160-, 80-, and 40-acre parcels. After all the allotments had been divvied out, the remaining lands were thrown open to non-Native homesteaders. One of the most damning legacies of the individualization of the Native lands was that as successive generations of Native heirs inherited allotments, the parcels became so splintered—fractionated—that multiple, sometimes hundreds, of individual interests were ultimately attached to single parcels, precluding any kind of sustainable development of the acreage.

Since the land was in trust status, however, it only rarely was alienated. Thus, the fractionation problem multiplied enormously. Although the allotment policy was ended in 1934 with the enactment of the Indian Reorganization Act, this did not prevent the compounding of the existing heirship problems, since each property owner was likely to have more than one heir. Studies conducted by both the House and Senate in 1960 showed that one-half of the approximately 12 million acres of allotted trust lands were held in fractionated ownership, with more than 3 million acres held by more than six heirs to a parcel.

In November 1974, Deloria wrote a letter to Donna Crossland in which he took on the issue of heirship. He opined that this was a topic to which he had given a great deal of thought, and, as the issue was terribly complex, he indicated it needed to be addressed forcefully because "some 150,000 acres of land had been returned to tribes [since 1966] and [yet] they have probably lost about 400,000 acres of allotted lands in that time."[107] He then identified the different types of Native land and gave examples of Native peoples holding particular lands in heirship, including grazing lands (tribal nations in Montana and the Dakotas), timber lands (Native peoples in Washington, Oregon, Wisconsin), irrigated farming lands (Native nations in Idaho, Arizona, New Mexico), commercial areas (tribal nations in Palm Springs; Fort Hall, Utah; various Pueblos communities), mineral lands (several Native peoples in Oklahoma, the Northern Cheyenne, Crow of Montana), and waterfront recreation properties (the Flathead Nation, Lummi Nation, Colville people).

He then offered suggestions for how Native peoples holding particular types of heirship lands could confront and resolve the issue. For example, for those nations with waterfront recreation properties, such as the Lummi people and the Shoalwater community, he suggested the "creation of a corporation of all commercially feasible lands for the small tribes … and a series of corporations by location for the larger tribes…. The shareholders would be the present owners of their lands—excluding a life estate for the present owners—and their present heirs would receive a distribution of stock at par value of a dollar per share wherever they are eligible." Finally, "the property of the corporation would be managed by a person hired by the stockholders and probably leased to the tribe if an enterprise was wanted."[108]

Deloria felt the category of timberlands would be the most difficult to tackle "because the lands are worth millions—some trees are now worth $15,000 each so we cannot talk about consolidation by purchase in any sense." "I would suggest," he said, that a community of cutting units be established which would contain a minimum number of allottees and be not more than 10,000 acres per unit. Tribal governments should be reorganized to represent these units economically and the tribe would resemble a nation more than a reservation with representation from each unit. The present allotments, which are about 80 acres each, should be broken down by survey into 10 acre plots by each community so that the maximum number of interests are realized for indefinite tracts of land and a general plan for cutting the timber systematically and under sustained yield should be created. The normal 10% fee charged by the BIA should be returned to a general community fund and used to manage the forest and to purchase any shares which would, upon the death of an allottee, fall to their heir under a certain value.[109]

He noted that his timber plan would be viewed negatively by a variety of groups, including individual Native heirs, whom he believed would complain that reduced acreage would lead to reduced profits. Still, he felt his 10 percent plan would ultimately benefit both the Native heirs and the land itself. "Sustained yield and reforestation would be much easier with 10 acre tracts and that would make forest management a much more scientific affair plus a community affair." Importantly, Deloria emphasized, the ten-acre tracts would also be better shielded from exploitation by timber companies because "it would be more difficult for a timber company to get a hold of Indian timber lands if they had to purchase 10 acres at a time rather than 80 acres at a time and if they had to deal with a minimum of 10 community political groups rather than a subcommittee of the tribal council."[110]

With regards to irrigated and commercial areas, Deloria recommended creation of a corporation led by a manager from outside the area. That person would be subject to federal Indian law and policy, but would be authorized to broker, sell, or trade lands. The corporate manager would also be responsible, under the auspices of federal law, to expand the reservation's boundaries "wherever he could best develop and expand" the lands. The "holders of interests would be given proportionate shares in a general closed corporation with the shares figured so that any immediate determination of estates could be handled easily by division of the shares of each interest holder."[111] Deloria stressed that this corporation would not be a holding corporation but an acquisition corporation.

He gave as one example the Salt River Pima-Maricopa reservation near Phoenix, Arizona. Here is the scenario he laid out:

> The corporation would sell the lands on the west side of the reservation where the Scottsdale bankers are ready to purchase at some $1000 a front foot and it would purchase lands on the east and north which are much less valuable now but which will eventually be worth a great deal in 50 years if the growth continues as it has. The reservation communities could be established with new housing on the newly purchased lands and people could take their interests in lands. For example, if a person has a 1/1,000th interest in a 10 acre lot worth $500,000 he could exchange his interest for about 2 acres worth $250 per acre on the side of the reservation. In other words, you are trading extremely valuable land in which a person might have an infinitesimal but valuable interest in commercial land for lands much further away from the urban expansion and get much more.[112]

Some progress has been made on fractionated heirship lands, as evidenced by federal and Native property activities that were instituted under the *Cobell* class action lawsuit/settlement that was settled in 2009. The plan provided $2 billion for the purchase of small, fractionated interests of Native landowners on a voluntary basis. Since 2013 the Department of the Interior reports that the federal government's Land Buy-Back Program for Tribal Nations has paid nearly $715 million to landowners to purchase their fractional interests. The Buy-Back Program has been funded through 2022, as there are some 245,000 owners of nearly 3 million fractional interests that are eligible to participate.[113]

Tests of Utmost Good Faith

In an interview with staff of *Akwesasne Notes* in 1975, Deloria detailed several specific ideas that, if ever embraced, would go far toward addressing the problematic Indigenous situation he had outlined in *The Indian Affair*. To date, none of these have been fully acted upon, yet it is evident that they remain the vortex of what needs to be repaired if Native political, legal, and territorial status is to be clarified and solidified. These are the identified needs:

- A "precise definition of the status and political identity of Indian communities."[114]

- A clear definition of the legal relationship between the United States and the Native nations. (Note: This would prevent, or at least forestall, efforts by courts, states, and the federal government to try to take or diminish Native lands or resources simply because those polities wanted them.)

- Build upon one of "the clearest and most traditional doctrines of law: one cannot imply a treaty abrogation, a change of status, or intent of Congress with respect to Indians unless it is clearly, explicitly, and specifically spelled out."[115]

- Clarify Native title to land and natural resources. Native peoples "still have a nebulous title to our land which goes back to the 1500s and the basis of this is that because Indians were not Christian, we had no capability of ever holding good land title."[116] This may well be the single most important problem Indigenous peoples still endure under federal law. Deloria strongly believed in the need for a "new status for Indian lands today." Realizing the improbability of the federal government simply conceding full fee-simple title to tribal nations, he posited that political-economic entities like the Tennessee Valley Authority, Ports of Authority, and other agencies had an ownership status of lands that might usefully serve as "models" for Native nations and the Congress to consider. "We must," observed Deloria, "use those agencies as models, and get a clear and simple definition from the Congress concerning our lands—and this must be done quickly."[117]

- Rein in the vast discretionary power of the secretary of interior and his/her subordinates over the use and regulation of Native lands, waters, and other resources owned by Native nations but largely controlled by the Interior department.

- Address the near-jurisdictional anarchy that did and still does prevail in Indian Country. Deloria identified a simple and historically, legally sound way to resolve this: "Unless a state or the federal government can show a specific grant of jurisdictional powers from the Indian tribe concerned to that government, there is no state or federal jurisdiction that can be exercised against the Indian tribe."[118]

- Related to the issue of jurisdiction, Deloria revived an idea that John Collier, former commissioner of Indian Affairs, had first voiced in the early stages of his tenure in 1934—the need for a permanent Court of Indian Affairs that would hear all suits involving Native nations.[119]

Also in 1975, Deloria published an op-ed in the *Los Angeles Times* titled "Federal Policy Still Victimizes and Exploits,"[120] wherein he pointedly observed that while Native activists sometime distorted issues or facts in their zeal to communicate with the public, "one can only note that federal officials have consistently distorted contemporary realities as a matter of policy." He continued by asking a seminal question: "What, then is the State of Indian nations in this summer of our continuing discontent?" Here he described the FBI's misconduct focused on AIM and its two most famous leaders—Dennis Banks and Russell Means.

He also described the many deaths of Natives on the Pine Ridge Reservation in South Dakota that had not been thoroughly investigated by the FBI, even though that agency is charged by law with investigating all major crimes in Indian Country.

He went on to criticize the US Congress for refusing to develop substantive reforms, even though the so-called Abourezk Commission (named after Senator James Abourezk [SD]), formed in 1975 in response to the explosion of Indigenous activism and demonstrations across the country, was supposed to be the mechanism for the adoption and implementation of needed reforms. The BIA was also attacked for continuing to treat Native governments as incipient bodies in perpetual need of federal supervision. And he also chided the National Congress of American Indians for having been "corrupted by large federal grants which make them supporters of federal policy rather than independent critics of its lethargy." Deloria ended the piece by darkly noting that, "unless the [federal] bureaucrats are brought to account, who knows what violence we can expect."[121]

In 1976, Deloria contributed a piece titled "The Twentieth Century" to an edited volume called *Red Men and Hat Wearers: Viewpoints in Indian History*.[122] In it he proposed a resolution for the Black Hills land issue that had dogged Lakota-US relations for more than a century. He thought the federal government should set up a special commission tasked to determine the legality of the "taking" of the Black Hills and proscribe an appropriate land restoration and financial compensation package for the Lakota. Always aware of the importance of historical precedent, he astutely suggested that the federally established Pueblo Lands Act of 1924, which created a board to ascertain which Pueblo lands had been illegally taken or squatted on by non-Pueblos, was an excellent example of a model that had brought some finality to the legitimate land rights of the Pueblo communities.[123]

The Western Shoshone were another Native nation whose particular land struggles were the focus of several of Deloria's more case-oriented analyses, in part because their property losses have been profound despite the laws and treaties that support their rights to their aboriginal territory. It is a struggle that continues to this day. In a brief essay in 1976 titled "The Western Shoshone,"

Deloria urged that individuals and governments interested in justice should closely examine the struggles the traditional Western Shoshone were then experiencing via the Indian Claims Commission (ICC) and Congress. He proposed that the ICC should be fully reviewed with an eye to determining "whether the Investigative Division has fulfilled the intent of the law by researching and investigating the Indian claims."[124]

In particular, Deloria urged an investigation of (1) papers filed by the Investigative Division, (2) evidence the division considered, and (3) conclusions the division made regarding tribal nations' present rights to lands, fishing rights, minerals, tax exemptions, and self-governance. The ICC formally ceased in 1978, leaving nearly eighty unresolved cases, all of which were transferred to the Court of Claims where many of them still languish.[125] The Western Shoshone, like many other Indigenous nations, still await a fair judgment of their claims against the United States.

In 1977, Deloria was invited by Leslie W. Dunbar, executive director of the Field Foundation, to write an occasional paper examining a "national question" and to make recommendations on how to improve the status and rights of the affected group in question. Deloria's submission was aptly called *A Better Day for Indians*. Before identifying and discussing seven major recommendations, Deloria first gave a concise comparison of Native peoples with other minorities and then, more importantly, shrewdly identified and analyzed what he termed the "seven controlling assumptions" or implied powers that provide Congress with enormous self-assumed power vis-à-vis Native nations.

These are the "assumptions" that generate federal attitudes, perceptions, and, of course, produce policies and laws that frequently debilitate the inherent sovereignty of tribal nations. First, there is an assumption that *"Congress is presumed to act in good faith toward Indians"* (emphasis his) and that Congressional members act in the "best interests" of Native people.[126] Deloria posited that this presumption was the most important of the seven he would be discussing "because it allows the federal government to disclaim any ultimate moral responsibility for its acts."[127] Thus, even poorly developed and weakly enforced laws and regulations are never properly evaluated.

Second, and evolving out of the first, is the presumption that past congressional policies are rooted in intelligent criteria that involve a solid understanding of tribal nations, and that these criteria have the consent of the affected Native communities. However, this has only sometimes been the case, as history amply shows. The third assumption, steeped in federal paternalism, is that answers to Indian "problems" are almost invariably conceived as mere adjustments to preexisting programs. Fourth, there is an assumption that Native homelands are human laboratories where social engineers can try out their ideas on the willing Indigenous populations. The General Allotment Act, boarding schools, and the "termination" of certain Native communities were for some congressional and BIA officials social, cultural, and economic experiments to test social theories of social Darwinism.[128]

Fifth, there has long been an assumption, backed by military force and law, that the United States retains the right to use Native lands at its own discretion. Sixth, there is an implicit attitude that the separation of powers doctrine and checks and balances theory, which generally works fairly well to protect the basic constitutional rights of most American citizens, are largely ineffective in protecting tribal sovereignty or treaty rights. This is because historically the three branches have typically acted in lockstep when they seek to diminish Native rights, or one or more branches will acquiesce or defer to the other branches without stepping in to investigate what has transpired.

Finally, there is a belief among state and local officials that "tribal rights are nuisances that can be abated as needs be."[129] This is glaringly evident today in the manner in which many state governors and legislators behave toward Native nations with successful gaming operations. In a number of instances, these officials, ignoring the fact that gaming proceeds are supposed to be used to benefit tribal governments and their economic and political development aspirations, are pressuring those nations to renegotiate compacts, threatening to tax tribal gaming revenues, or are pushing them to surrender ever more of their proceeds to state coffers.[130] Increasingly, there are conflicts over environmental questions when states or other entities fail to consult tribes before proceeding with development or other plans that affect treaty rights.

With these federal assumptions as a critical, if not always self-evident, reality, Deloria then discussed seven specific recommendations.[131] Several of these had appeared in some of his earlier works, but here they were brought together to form a comprehensive package. He urged the following:

1. A uniform recognition of Indigenous communities (federal recognition for all bona fide tribal groups).

2. A clarification of tribal membership (updated and verifiable tribal rolls).

3. A standard definition of the status of a Native nation.

4. The creation of a permanent Court of Indian Affairs.

5. Arbitration and just settlement of long-standing land and trust-fund claims (e.g., Black Hills, Western Shoshone, etc.).

6. Rejuvenation of the Native land base (fractionated lands, in particular, need to be forcefully addressed and consolidated).

7. Universal eligibility for government aid based on need.

Deloria acknowledged in his conclusion that this was an ambitious and even "controversial" set of recommendations, but he believed that his "organically related" set of reforms would, if enacted, have a dramatically positive affect on the current situations of Indigenous peoples.[132]

To date, Congress has only acted directly on one of these suggestions, number 6. The Indian Land Consolidation Act was first enacted in 1983,[133] and through it tribal governments were authorized, with the approval of the secretary of interior, "to adopt a land consolidation plan providing for the sale or exchange of any tribal lands or interest in lands for the purposes of eliminating individual fractional interests in Indian trust or restricted lands or consolidating its tribal land holdings."[134] The act was challenged in federal court, however, on the grounds that the escheat provision was "an unconstitutional taking of private property,"[135] which led to congressional amendments to the law.[136] Importantly, as noted earlier, the *Cobell* class action settlement of 2009 contained provisions—including setting aside 2 billion dollars for the purchase of fractionated interests—that have begun to pay dividends insofar as consolidating the fractionated land base. The process has thus improved, but is still far from resolved.

Support for Eastern Native Nations

In the fall of 1977, Deloria was tapped by members of the Mashpee Wampanoag to serve as an expert witness in a case, *Mashpee Tribe v. New Seabury Corp*,[137] originally filed in 1976 by the Wampanoag against a group of non-Indian landowners living in the town of Mashpee, Massachusetts. The Wampanoag sought to use the federal Non-Intercourse Act, first enacted in 1790 and reenacted several times until it was codified in 1834, to argue that their land had been purchased illegally because the federal government had not overseen the property transaction.

But at the time of the trial in 1977, the Wampanoag were not yet recognized by the federal government as a bona fide tribal entity. Thus, this first trial was conducted to determine the legal "status" of the Wampanoags at the time of the lawsuit and when the land transactions had taken place. When Deloria was called to testify on November 9, 1977, he was compelled to prove he was competent as an expert witness. After providing his academic credentials, he was asked by an attorney what types of documentary studies had he generated in the past. Deloria's answer was a compelling statement on his methodology:

> Well, you don't really study tribes. You work with the people to help them prepare the best understanding you can of what the current problems are, how they got in the situation they got into. In the course of that you talk with a great many Indians. A lot of times they

remember things that are not in the ordinary train of documents that your standard economic scholar would run across. So in checking the oral testimony, the oral tradition of the people, then that gives you additional leads as to where you can find other sources to fill in the history. And there is no really good history on any tribe in the country. You have to do this process with every group you meet.[138]

Here we see a clear indication of the amount of respect Deloria had for Indigenous oral tradition and his willingness to directly interface with people and not alleged "experts."

In a follow-up question, he was asked to estimate the number of Native peoples he had researched. "I would say in the neighborhood of fifty tribes," Deloria replied. And he pointed out that these were distinct Native communities, including more than fifteen Lakota and Dakota reservations; the Nooksack, Lummi, Quinault, and Puyallup of Washington State; the Klamath of Oregon; the Crow of Montana; the Seneca of New York; the Payson Apache of Arizona; the Tunica-Biloxi of Louisiana; the Ottawa and Pottawatomie of Michigan; and the Lumbee of North Carolina.[139]

Later during his testimony Deloria was asked by the presiding judge, "Can you tell us what criteria you use to identify an Indian community as a tribe?" Deloria responded, "As I use it and as I understand other Indian people using it, it means a group of people living pretty much in the same place who know who their relatives are. And I think that's the basic way we look at things. You can add or subtract all kinds of footnotes if you want, but I think that would be the generally acceptable way Indians would look at it. That's the way I look at it."[140]

Deloria's definition failed to satisfy the attorney for the opposing side, who latched on to the fact that he had not mentioned political organization as a requisite criterion in his definition. But Deloria deftly emphasized that Native peoples also typically had institutional structures that could at least loosely be compared to the social, political, and economic categories of most Western societies, and the judge chided the opposing lawyer for "trying to lead [Deloria] by the nose into judicial definitions, somewhat against his will." The Wampanoag failed to convince the jury that they were a "tribe," but thirty years later, in 2007, they were finally admitted to the ranks of federally recognized tribal entities.[141]

Recognizing Traditions as Common Sense

Sometime in early 1977 Deloria concluded a position paper that had been requested by a group of traditional individuals from various Native nations, including members of the Lakota Treaty Council of Rapid City, South Dakota, and the Onondaga Council of Chiefs of the Iroquois Confederacy. They had asked him to produce a statement that reflected their views on sovereignty, treaty rights, and other issues they hoped might culminate in a high-level meeting with President Jimmy Carter and Vice President Walter Mondale.

Deloria produced a ten-page document that he titled "Traditional Indian Position Paper." The work provided a precise overview of the complicated and lengthy relationship between Indigenous peoples and non-Natives, explained why there was such unrest in Indian Country, and laid out a broad suggestion for a meeting that he hoped would begin the process of addressing the concerns of these traditional-minded citizens.[142]

After identifying many of the federal government's major treaty and human rights violations, treaty abuses, and policy blunders dating from the last formal treaties negotiated in 1868, Deloria suggested that "all of these policies, programs, and failures occurred because after 1871[143] the federal government and the courts held to the doctrine that Indians should not and could not have political status to negotiate with the United States as equals as they had done during the previous century. Policies were made for Indians, not by or with them."[144]

For Deloria and the traditionalists he was writing to represent, the solution lay in the formal resuscitation of the treaty process.

The traditional people once again, in this paper, presented to the White House, the invitation to sit down and begin prolonged and serious discussions on the state of Indian affairs, seeking a new mechanism whereby Indians can be brought into the process of solving problems of long-standing. The traditional people believe that only in an extended conversation which covers the points in dispute between the United States and the Tribes can any progress be made in solving problems. Not only must policy be discussed but agreements must be reached concerning the resolution of historic and contemporary conflicts.[145]

Upon completion of the document, Deloria presented it to Louis Bad Wound (Lakota) and Chief Irving Powless Jr. (Onondaga), who then distributed it to the members of both their parties. On February 4, 1977, Chief Powless, on behalf of the traditional group members, including Deloria, wrote a letter to Richard Moe Esquire, assistant to the vice president, requesting a meeting. Powless made a point of noting that "the BIA does not speak for nor reflect the perspective of Traditional Native Americans; that the National Tribal Chairmen's Association more often reflects Bureau policy; and that the National Congress of American Indians even in the light of its currently changing attitude of becoming more supportive of Traditional views and treaties, still cannot present our perspectives or represent us."[146]

In August 1977, Deloria penned another op-ed to the *Los Angeles Times* titled "...But What of Human Rights for U.S. Indians,"[147] in which he urged President Jimmy Carter to focus attention on the ongoing difficulties that Native peoples still endured in the United States, particularly the extremely high death rate by questionable means in Indian Country, including the forced sterilization of thousands of Native women by Indian Health Clinic doctors. He chided Carter for paying more attention to human rights in foreign nations than in his own backyard. He urged the president to "provide ethical leadership for his administration in its dealings with Indians. More significant than any new program or specific policy change introduced by the President will be the moral tone he sets."[148]

In 1980, the US Supreme Court handed down a major decision regarding Lakota land rights, *United States v. Sioux Nation*.[149] The 8–1 decision (Rehnquist dissented) affirmed a Court of Claims decision that ordered the federal government to pay eight Native nations $105 million as part of the compensation for the federal government's illegal taking of the Black Hills of South Dakota in 1877. Deloria wrote a short essay about the case titled "Like the Victory Over Custer, the Sioux's Legal Win Can Mean Defeat."[150] In the piece he provided a succinct summary of the case, but he noted that even with this victory the battle was far from over because Congress would still have to appropriate the funds, there would need to be tribal referenda to decide on how to spend the money, discussion would need to occur about who would be eligible for the money (creation of a tribal roll), and the people would have to decide whether or not to divide the money on a per capita basis. Finally, the Congress would then have to approve the manner in which the Natives decided to use the money.

Having observed what transpired in other Native communities that received large financial claims settlements, Deloria worried that the burdens of arriving at the decision as to who was eligible for benefits would prove especially daunting and divisive. He was also aware that the nations and their members would be subject to the corrosive entreaties of "drug dealers, bootleggers, used car dealers, and appliance salesmen who would ordinarily cross the street to avoid saying hello to an Indian,"[151] all with designs on how they might exploit the newfound wealth.

Deloria urged the tribal nations' leaders and citizens, however, to look ahead and to think, as Red Cloud had done upon signing the 1868 treaty: "How will my actions affect seven generations of Lakota?" Deloria implored the nations to use the money "to purchase lands within and adjoining the existing reservation and in the Black Hills and resettling people on economical tracts where they can at least enjoy the subsistence life of farming and ranching that has been their fate since 1877."[152]

Anticipating some of the most difficult problems that Native nations are now having over wealth distribution from gambling enterprises as well as impacts to citizenship, Deloria was most concerned about the possibility that the nations might decide to rely on per capita distribution of much of the financial award. "Per capita distribution and the subsequent expenditure of over $100 million on consumer goods, however, would be a clear signal that the Sioux people have adopted the white man's wasteful ways, and demand everything now in defiance of their responsibilities to coming generations."[153] He concluded that, "losing the case would have kept the tribe together in their persistent struggle to make the government return the Black Hills." Interestingly, the Lakota, despite their profound poverty, refused to accept the financial award received in US v. Sioux Nation, and they continue to do so. The original figure of $105 million, with compounding interest, now exceeds more than $1.2 billion. Raymond Orr's 2017 study, Reservation Politics, which includes a detailed examination of the Lakota land issue, concluded that their "strong opposition to any deal and the absence of an additional settlement for the last thirty years is clear evidence that the community is not looking for or expecting greater compensation short of the return of the Black Hills to its ownership."[154]

Meeting of the Minds

A strong advocate of interdisciplinarity, Deloria spent several years in the early 1980s working with Cecil Corbett, then at the Cook Christian Training School, to organize a conference intended to pull together a small but diverse group of lawyers, theologians, philosophers, and traditional Native citizens. The goal was to collaborate on the formulation of fresh concepts and a broader and deeper understanding of the theoretical, philosophical, and practical intergovernmental relationships between Native nations and other polities as well as with the larger society.

In his invitation letter to the dedicated activist and attorney John Petoskey of the National Indian Youth Council (NIYC) in November 1983, Deloria put it this way:

About ten years ago Cecil Corbett and I began discussing how the framework could be established for an Indian litigation program that would lead to important and irreversible victories and confirmation of Indian rights. We took as a starting point the fact that Black victories had been possible because the logic of their claims made sense in both theological and legal terms—the brotherhood of man being the theological expression of legal equality, integration being full participation in the community, and so forth. There are a number of critical concepts within the Indian field which have counterparts in theological language—treaty and covenant for example, which it has seemed to us are critical to any future understanding of Indian issues and any solution to them.[155]

The conference, titled "Indian Law and Theology Symposium," was held in December 1983 at Princeton University. In addition to Deloria and Corbett, participants included Harold Berman (constitutional lawyer), John Petoskey (Native lawyer), James Cone (professor of theology), Jack Greenberg (NAACP lawyer), Gerald One Feather (Lakota, chief of police at Pine Ridge Reservation), Oren Lyons (Onondaga chief), Milner Ball (constitutional lawyer), Paul Lehmann (theologian), Tim Coulter (lawyer), and Christopher Stone (constitutional lawyer).

In advance of the gathering, Deloria had written a prospectus that served as a backdrop for discussion. He observed that Native nations needed the support of both theological leaders and the legal profession in their efforts to properly frame their moral and legal claims against the federal government and American society. He noted that the most intractable and damning political and legal issue confronting tribal nations was the omnipresent plenary power doctrine that places Indian people "at the complete mercy of Congress and the respective executive administrations ... because it situates Indian people and their treaty and trust resources and rights outside the reach of constitutional protections."[156]

Deloria was emphatic that this doctrine must be overturned or at least radically altered through a "gradual process involving a series of law cases in which the Supreme Court carefully thinks out, step by step, the implications of the idea that Indians constitute a separate political entity protected by the federal government but not subject to its internal political changes."[157]

Also in 1983, Deloria coauthored the first of two books with a political science colleague, Clifford M. Lytle, titled *American Indians, American Justice.* It was the first comprehensive text devoted to exploring the unique evolution and status of tribal governments, with special emphasis on the judicial arms of these polities. The study also contained valuable information about the tribal-federal political and legal relationship and the role that law and lawyers play in intergovernmental affairs.

Deloria and Lytle observed that some of the problems between Native nations and the federal government were "structural" in nature. In other words:

> Many of the legal problems that tribes need to resolve are directed to the Solicitor's Office in the Department of the Interior, and the associate solicitor for Indian affairs assumes a prominent role in settling these legal issues. The solicitor, like the Bureau of Indian Affairs, should theoretically be an advocate for the tribal governments. But the Indian tribes are his or her particular clients only with respect to issues involving parties outside the Department of the Interior; with respect to issues between agencies of the department, the solicitor theoretically has the department as his or her client and must determine a course of action that will produce internal satisfaction. Thus, the solicitor can become an advocate in the first discussion of the issues involving Indians. Not infrequently, Indian tribal governments and/or the BIA come into conflict with other agencies housed within Interior, such as the Bureau of Reclamation and the Bureau of Land Management. The solicitor thus may represent multiple clients who frequently possess antagonistic interests. In private practice this representation would give rise to an unethical situation in which the attorney's license would be jeopardized. But

instead of facing up to the ethical dilemma, at times the Solicitor's Office will simply attempt to bring about an accommodation of the conflicting interests and quite often this accommodation will be purchased at the cost of enforcing Indian rights.[158]

Until this structural and ethical dilemma is resolved, tribal nations will sometimes find their rights being subsumed or overridden, rather than properly enforced.

Second, Deloria and Lytle acknowledged another difficult situation that Indigenous peoples confront. This one centers on a power the secretary of interior had held since the Indian Reorganization Act of 1934—the power to approve or disapprove of any agreement entered into between individual lawyers and Native governments. As they noted, "It is a blatant violation of the notion that everyone, including Indian tribes, should possess freedom of choice in selecting legal representation."

Congress modified this in 1988, although it still allowed too much discretionary and paternalistic power to reside in the Interior Department. But on March 14, 2000, Congress enacted the Indian Tribal Economic Development and Contract Encouragement Act of 2000.[159] Although the act retained in the role of secretary the authority to approve of agreements or contracts with the Five Civilized Tribes or agreements that encumber Indian land for seven or more years, it, for the first time, denied the secretary the power to approve contracts for legal services provided by attorneys to Native nations in general. The only exception allowed is the secretary's ability to retain this power over attorneys' contracts if a tribe's constitution contains express language calling for such overview.

A year later, Deloria and Lytle produced their second book, *The Nations Within* (1984). This impressive work was really two books in one. The first half constituted a splendid policy analysis of the IRA. The last contained a detailed set of recommendations for the federal government and tribal nations. The federal reforms were included in chapter 17, appropriately titled "The Future of Indian Nations." The authors laid out a comprehensive package of four broad but interrelated reforms.

The first two reforms spoke directly to tribal nations, and will be addressed in chapter 3. But the final two, while implicating Natives, were aimed specifically at the federal government: (1) the need for Native governments to attain economic stability and (2) the need for stabilization in the political relationship between the federal, state, and tribal governments, which could only be attained by "mutual respect and parity" in political relations.[160]

Deloria and Lytle argued that Native governments, in their efforts to establish economic stability, faced a frustrating and desperate situation, given the long history of federal efforts to acquire or control Native lands and resources. Here, the two scholars reiterated a point Deloria had made throughout his career: that until Native land ownership was fully recognized and the allotted lands and heirship problems addressed, land consolidation would remain "the major unsolved economic problem of Indian tribes." As the writers graphically observed: "Until tribes are able to own their own lands in one solid block, they cannot reasonably make plans for use or development of their resources. But consolidation has other implications that make it important. Civil and criminal jurisdiction depends upon the existence of trust lands."[161]

At a more fundamental level, Deloria and Lytle stressed that the issue of tribal economic stability could only be resolved if the BIA and tribal officials were able to effectively settle the dilemma of whether Native land was a commodity to be exploited as a corporate type of property, or whether it was to be viewed and treated as the tribal nations' homeland "in which case it assumes a mystical focal point for other activities that support the economic stability of the reservation society."[162]

Regarding stabilization of the intergovernmental relationship between Native governments, the federal government, and states, Deloria and Lytle again emphasized the need to respect and restart the treaty process. They also suggested that rather than litigating intergovernmental conflicts with the states and the national government, "the idea of arbitration and mediation," which traditional Native people support, is a more realistic way to manage political and legal differences.[163] In fact, there is some evidence that arbitration, mediation, and negotiation are catching on, especially in Native nation-state relations.[164] For example, several state governors, beginning in the late 1980s and continuing to the present, have signed "sovereignty accords" with the Native nations they share borders with, accentuating that the government-to-government relationship between the two parties should be based on a mutual respect for the sovereignty of each other.[165]

Finally, Deloria and Lytle encouraged states and Indigenous leaders to continue their efforts to achieve a full faith and credit relationship. This would mean, at a minimum, that the basic treaty relationship would have to be accepted by the states, which sometimes struggle with the concept of according any recognition or legitimacy to Native governments.[166]

Also in 1984, Deloria coedited a book with Sandra L. Cadwalader titled *The Aggressions of Civilization: Federal Indian Policy Since the 1880s*.[167] Deloria also contributed an essay to the book, "Congress in Its Wisdom: The Course of Indian Legislation," an analysis of the rationale and type of laws Congress has enacted involving Indian affairs. In his conclusion he discussed a little known congressional law, the Indian Delegation Act of 1946,[168] wherein Congress gave the Department of Interior authority to delegate administrative responsibility to lower-level federal employees.

Deloria believed that "this substantially diluted the trust responsibility of the department. In effect, Congress washed its hands of Indians and assumed that Indian matters could be handled administratively. Thereafter, the information that Congress received regarding Indians was carefully screened by the Interior Department, and of course represented the bureaucratic view of things."[169] While not directly suggesting that Congress should override or amend this law, there was a sense in this writing that, unless legislative changes were made, the BIA and the interior secretary would continue to wield far more explicit and discretionary power over tribal nations than they are constitutionally entitled to with Congress's express acquiescence.

The notion of this being a "gradual process" rooted in educational transformation rather than a radical or immediate one was important for Deloria, for he feared that the American public might raise vigorous objections if the changes came too quickly. In a comparison with African Americans during the civil rights era, he observed that too often many non-Natives ask why Natives want to be "different," when the more appropriate question should be why Native people do not enjoy the right to be distinctive.

In 1987, during congressional testimony at a hearing on a proposed Senate concurrent resolution to acknowledge the importance of Haudenosaunee (Iroquois) democratic traditions and theory on the development of the US Constitution, Deloria discussed several key directives that he wanted Congress to draft to sincerely demonstrate greater respect for the sovereignty of Native nations.[170] These would be directives, he urged, that should be binding on each branch of the government, particularly the federal courts.

First, he said that the most critical piece should be a statement from Congress that national legislation is inapplicable to Native nations unless they are expressly included in the legislation.[171] Then, Congress needed to statutorily declare that Indigenous peoples must give their unequivocal consent before any federal program is instituted in Indian Country or that in any way directly affects Native rights.[172] At the present time, Deloria observed, tribal governments, despite their inherent powers of sovereignty and self-determination, lacked the recognized capacity to reject or veto secretarial rules or regulations or congressional acts if they found them objectionable. This inherent power is lacked by tribal governments to this day.

The third and capstone directive, one that Deloria urged from the beginning of his storied career, is that Congress should categorically state that Native treaties establish not only a unique legal but also a moral relationship between tribal nations and the United States and, in substance, entail "a pledge of the integrity of one people to another."[173]

Given the generally dishonorable way the United States had enforced treaties over time, Deloria asserted that it was time that Congress conduct oversight hearings on all the major programs the federal bureaucracy carried out on behalf of Native nations. In addition, he urged that Congress hold hearings on the Indian Claims Commission and the problems generated under the American Indian Religious Freedom Act of 1978.

Lessons from a Scout for the Nations

In 1988, as I entered my second year of graduate school at the University of North Carolina at Chapel Hill, I began to ponder dissertation topics. In April of that year I wrote Deloria, and he replied with a detailed letter identifying several potential issues that warranted consideration. They still do, so I will share them here.

He commenced with a topic that he had already begun to wrestle with—looking to find an analogous relationship between Native governments and the federal government that would be of benefit to all parties. "One intriguing thought, to me," he said,

> is a theme which I developed when I was trying to do an essay on the Constitution for the Iroquois. I said that the treaty/trust relationship was comparable in most respects to the 10th amendment which reserves to the states certain powers that they do not cede to the federal government. Posing the question in that manner would elevate the treaty into a reasonably powerful document within the framework of the Constitution and American history and would then suggest that seeking the consent of the tribes for legislation is a necessity and not a concession.[174]

He explained this could be demonstrated quite easily by the practical manner in which the US Congress acts when it contacts tribal governments in advance of major legislation, or as when a sitting president, Richard Nixon, once phoned the leadership of the Alaska Federation of Natives and asked whether he should sign the Alaska Native Claims Settlement Act.

Deloria even laid out a methodological approach for me to consider. He suggested preparing a questionnaire and then attending a National Congress of American Indians annual convention to ask Native delegates to fill out the questionnaires about the current state of Native-state relations that would "show that states are held back from interfering with the tribes in certain areas and in those areas federal officials quite often defer to tribal sovereignty. So there are areas where Native/state relations are deadlocked and always will be because each sovereign has inherent powers that are complete."[175]

His second research idea delved into political philosophy. He suggested that I "pose the question of whether or not the U.S. has abided by its promise in the [1787] Northwest Ordinance [by] exercising the utmost good faith towards Indians." This could be accomplished by "examining the major pieces of congressional legislation and in particular policy amendments in Indian appropriation acts to show that in most cases there is no 'wisdom' of Congress—everything is helter-skelter and ad hoc because a senator or congressman can change certain things whenever it suits their interest."[176]

Finally, he broached the subject of urban Natives, a topic that remains fraught with difficulty for tribal governments, the federal government, and, of course, those Native individuals who migrated, or were forced to migrate, to metropolitan areas. With more than 60 percent of Native citizens living in or near cities, this issue begs for greater research. And while several case studies have been written about Natives in cities such as Albuquerque, Chicago, and San Francisco, not enough comprehensive data has been generated that might culminate in productive policies at either the federal or tribal level. Deloria's suggestion to me was to "examine how an urban Indian center for instance operates on federal grants," and he said I should "take the proposition that the treaty relationship and/or trust relationship is with the tribal nation, not individual groups of people, and that consequently there should be regular appropriations for the urban population because they are also tribal members." In Deloria's view, "responsibility is national and does not really depend on the reservation status. You would thereby restrict certain kinds of federal powers to situations in which there was a question of using natural resources that were held in trust."[177]

Two months after I had written back and suggested a different dissertation topic that would instead focus on a select group of US Supreme Court opinions dealing with the doctrines of federal plenary power and tribal sovereignty, Deloria responded by noting, "I don't know that analyzing twenty Supreme Court cases would do much of anything—it would depend on which cases you would take. But there are probably not enough good cases dealing with treaties—where the Indian tribe is a plaintiff—to make it worth your while." He then amended my idea and suggested what ultimately became my dissertation focus:

> You might want to zero in on a particular Supreme Court era—1885–1907—for example—and combine that with the then popular notion of the ending of the frontier in 1890 and see what the court did to Tribal-Federal relations. There are some startling decisions during those days—*Winans*,[178] *Winters*,[179] *Quick Bear*,[180] *Lone Wolf*,[181] *Kagama*,[182] etc., and out of those cases would come a thesis that the court was seeking to finally resolve the Indian situation by ceding all kinds of power to the federal government—by default—whereas it was very hesitant in its civil rights cases, income tax cases, and interstate commerce cases to do the same thing."[183]

Here, Deloria was referring to the court's construction of the congressional plenary power doctrine which arose in *US v. Kagama* (1886) and then expanded in *Lone Wolf v. Hitchcock* (1903), which affords the Congress virtually carte blanche authority vis-à-vis Indigenous governments and their resources.

By August of 1989, as I was preparing to begin my dissertation, I was experiencing severe writer's block and I wrote Deloria soliciting his advice. He sent me a lengthy letter, chock-full of sage advice about the meaning of scholarship, the problem of presentism, and the need to write rather than to simply read and gather data. "Scholarship today," he said, "is a fiction…. People don't really look impartially at some body of material, analyze it, and then tell others what's there. Rather people get a half-assed idea and they start to gather data which will support that idea and then they reach conclusions about it and arrange all the evidence they can find to support their original idea."[184]

As for the serious problem of presentism, Deloria was forewarning me about the problems associated with the human propensity to rely on one's present-day perspective and to read that back into history. As he put it,

19th century people were not very much concerned with sovereignty, and if they were it was conceived in entirely different terms— primarily as to how much, if any, control over the political functioning of the tribes was necessary. Here they [federal officials] split into two camps—those allowing the Five Civilized Tribes and others, Quapaw, Osage, Wyandott, Seneca, et al., tribes with a reasonably long period of contact with whites— to have their own form of government, provided that form of government looked a great deal like the U.S. and its states. When they found tribes like the Sioux and Cheyenne they were puzzled and played the chiefs off against the people but when they ran into the Apaches and Navajos they were totally astounded and that's why they waged such vicious war against the Apaches—they could not believe there could be small independent and self-sufficient units of society in a desert region.[185]

Finally, Deloria suggested that I stop reading court cases and begin to write. "As you write," he noted,

you will find that your mind begins to function in a much different manner—you will begin to see things and understand them much better. You will also see the relationships that you are now trying to find with the computer. Not that a computer is bad—although I personally don't care for them—but they will only give you the structural similarities of the [court] cases—they will not deal with the substance of ideas. That you will have to find as you begin to write.[186]

Deloria elaborated on what he meant by the need to write rather than simply read for consumptive purposes:

The human mind is a strange instrument. You can fill it too full and then nothing much happens because it is confused and can't produce anything. When you're writing you are taking whatever is in the front of the brain and transferring it to paper—in other words, clearing it out so that new ideas can come forward. As the new ideas come forward you will find that those ideas that are naturally attached to the ones you have on paper will come forward of their own accord and present themselves and the more you write the better you will feel and the more you will understand.[187]

He then gave a personal example of his writing travails:

One time when I was writing *God is Red* I had something like 185 pages done but it just wasn't going the way I thought it should. So I burned the whole thing—on the premise that if I really knew the subject I could start from scratch again and do better—and I did. After that each chapter flowed quite naturally so that as I was writing one chapter I found my mind working on the next chapter and I didn't actually know what I was writing until I was done. In fact, the last couple chapters I rushed through so I could sit down and read what I had written. All this is to say that you may in fact be driving yourself crazy with your present approach to things. There is no way you can hold that much material in your mind at one time and you will begin to get frustrated that you are apparently not learning or remembering anything. Do you sometimes feel the task is too much? That's because you are stuffing the front of your brain with material that wants to come out and be on paper. So get it out there.[188]

Calling Washington to Account

In the early 1990s, there was discussion in Washington, D.C., about the need for a permanent National Indian Policy Research Institute that would provide policy research materials and capability to assist Native governments and federal officials charged with fulfilling the nation's treaty and trust commitments to Indigenous peoples. Popularly referred to as "think tanks," such institutes or centers could play a leading role in bringing together the leadership and resources needed to address the variegated problems still bedeviling Indigenous peoples.[189]

Although the institute was never formally established, in July 1992 Deloria testified before Congress in support of its creation. He stressed that it should focus on two broad arenas of research. Since the trust doctrine and treaties and agreements are the linchpins linking Native nations and the United States, he wanted the institute to start by focusing some of its research on the origins of these doctrines, their inconsistent application and enforcement, and on the ways specific rights and individual Native nations had been affected by their sporadic implementation.

He then envisioned the institute serving as a place where new technologies, discoveries, and fresh applications of "existing information about economic, environment, legal theory and education" could be applied and "futuristic speculations and modeling" charted out so that tribal governments could look far into the future in anticipation of possible developments rather than simply reacting day-to-day on immediate problems. For example, he noted that "as environmental concepts change we find new ways to use lands and natural resources, growing and marketing buffalo for example, and if we are to finally stabilize our communities and participate fully in American society, we must be able to relate to the most sophisticated part of that society as communities and individuals."[190] Such a futuristic orientation, while still steeped in Indigenous values and philosophies, highlights one of the real strengths of Deloria's approach.

In September 1992, Deloria teamed up with Suzan Shown Harjo, Raymond D. Apodaca, Norbert Hill Jr., Mateo Romero, William A. Means, and Manley A. Begay to petition the US Patent and Trademark Board to cancel the six trademarks allowing the Washington Redskins, a professional football team, to use the name "Redskins," a label viewed with derision by a vast majority of Native individuals and governments.[191] In 1999, the Trademark Trial and Appeal Board (TTAB) of the US Department of Commerce unanimously ruled in the Natives' favor. The Washington Redskins appealed this decision, and in 2003 the US District Court for the District of Columbia ruled in *Pro-Football v. Harjo* that the Board's finding of disparagement was "not supported by substantial evidence and must be reversed" and that the case had been filed after an undue delay.

In 2013, a younger set of Native plaintiffs filed another suit against the football team. In 2014, the TTAB voted to cancel the six trademarks, holding that the word *Redskins* was, in fact, a disparaging concept to many Natives. In July 2015, a federal district court affirmed the TTAB ruling and ordered the cancellation of the Redskins trademark registration. However, the ruling did not bar the team from using the Redskins name. The Washington Redskins appealed this decision, and in June 2017, in a separate case taken to the US Supreme Court by an Asian rock band, The Slants, the high court declared that a key section of a federal law, the 1946 Lanham Act, banning trademarks that "may disparage" people was a violation of the First Amendment. This was the section that the Native plaintiffs had relied upon in arguing that the Redskins should be stripped of its trademark registrations. As a result of this decision, the attorney representing the Natives realized their case was moot, and, for now, this twenty-five-year battle is over.[192]

This recent case and the fact that there are still numerous professional, college, and high school teams that use caricatured images of Indigenous peoples as "mascots" serves as a harsh reminder to Native peoples that their identity is still subject to exploitation and derogation by the public, corporate America, and local and state governments.

In late 1995, the 10th Circuit Court of Appeals handed down a decision involving treaty rights, *Crow Tribe of Indians and Thomas L. Ten Bear v. Repsis*,[193] one that dramatically revived a nearly century-old case, *Ward v. Racehorse*,[194] which had held that a state had authority to override a Shoshone-Bannock member's treaty right to hunt on tribal land. The court based its ruling of state jurisdiction over tribal treaty rights on the equal footing doctrine because there was no express reservation in Wyoming's admission act or the state constitution guaranteeing the Indians' hunting rights. *Race Horse* was thought to have been implicitly overruled by several later Supreme Court opinions,[195] but it was being reasserted in *Repsis*.

Deloria knew *Repsis* was a potential blockbuster case that, if taken on by the Supreme Court, might endanger all Native treaty rights and strengthen the state position vis-à-vis those rights. In January 1996, he wrote me and strongly encouraged me to consult with several Native lawyers to see about organizing a conference to address the content and potential scope of *Repsis*. He said that he had spent much of the day

> calling around to see if people were doing anything about it and, of course, the tribal chairmen are all worried about the budget and so don't realize the devastation that can ensue if the case goes to the U.S. Supreme Court. In short, Indians may have had it—this 'statehood' doctrine is wholly fictional as we all realize but with Republicans in power and the Supreme Court jammed with conservatives, federal Indian law looks to be screwed up until the next century—and I mean 2096.[196]

"In the old days," Deloria concluded, "I would have known the case was being pursued and NCAI [National Congress of American Indians] would have had some kind of brief in place to support the tribe." Deloria was incensed by the decision and Indian Country's slow response to it, noting that "most of my life's work is now down the drain and I had best get busy on my 'Creation' book because that would be all that would be left. Hopefully, I will have destroyed western science and religion about the time that Indian treaties are declared null and void—so it would be a draw."[197]

A few days later he wrote me again and encouraged me to reach out to several other Native law and social science faculty at the University of Arizona to "plan some kind of high level emergency conference on the present state of federal courts and the revival of outmoded and discredited case law and doctrines." He said he would be willing to send a "frantic" note to several individuals in order to raise money for the conference.[198]

The NCAI did finally respond to the need for concentrated attention on this topic, and in 2001, in partnership with the Native American Rights Fund (NARF), they created the Sovereignty Protection Initiative, an enterprise to address the "disastrous court opinions and legislative attacks on the status of tribal governments" that were then flowing from those branches of the federal government. The leaders of the two organizations structured the initiative with four major components: (1) the Tribal Supreme Court Project, (2) the Federal Judicial Selection Project, (3) the Education and Public Outreach Committee, and (4) the Legislative Committee.[199] The Supreme Court Project element was designed to help Native nations and individuals consider the implications of taking particular cases to the federal courts, and the joint partnership has made a substantial difference in the kinds of Indian law cases that are introduced into the federal courts.

In Defense of the Ancient One

In July 1996, very old skeletal remains—estimated at that time to be between 9,000 and 10,000 years old—were unearthed on the banks of the Columbia River. Dubbed "Kennewick Man," the discovery led to an intense conflict ensued between the Native nations of the region and the scientific community. The former insisted that the person's remains should be quickly reinterred after completion of proper ceremonies as authorized under the Native American Graves Protection and Repatriation Act of 1990 (NAGPRA), while the latter demanded that it be allowed by the Army Corps of Engineers—which claimed jurisdiction over the remains—to scientifically examine the bodies, despite Native objections and in the face of the explicit statutory language in NAGPRA.

Deloria felt compelled to step into the fray, and on September 24, 1997, he sent a letter accompanied by an eight-page report detailing his concerns to Brigadier General Robert G. Griffen, division commander of the Northwestern Division of the US Army Corps of Engineers. He wrote that since the controversy had "recently received immense press coverage, the net effect had been to paint American Indians as obstructing the progress of 'science' by opposing the destructive study of the remains."[200] Deloria suggested, however, that "much of this coverage, and the statements of some of the plaintiffs' scholars only serve to confuse the issue, making the repatriation of the human remains appear to be a wrongful step by the US Army Corps of Engineers."

He emphasized that his interest in this important issue was on behalf of his own nation, the Standing Rock Sioux, but also other Lakota peoples, and "more generally on behalf of all Indian tribes." In his estimation, if the scientists won in court then "anyone screaming 'science' with any kind of hodge-podge doctrinal theory could invade any Indian graveyard and begin destructive and sacrilegious excavations of any area they wished to use."[201]

His focused report was a point-by-point rebuttal of the arguments being used by the scientists clamoring to study the remains. They claimed their preliminary study revealed the person had

> a diet high in marine food, that he may have been a fisherman who ate a lot of salmon … he seems to have been a tall, good-looking man, slender and well-proportioned. Studies have shown that 'handsomeness' is largely the result of symmetrical features and good health, both of which Kennewick Man had. Archaeological finds of similar age in the area suggest that he was part of a small band of people who moved about, hunting, fishing, and gathering wild plants. He may have lived in a simple sewn tent or mat hut that could be disassembled and carried. Some nearby sites contain large numbers of fine bone needles, indicating that a lot of delicate sewing was going on.[202]

Deloria sharply questioned the veracity of these claims and asked the corps to consider the merit behind the scientists' assertions. He urged them to compel scientists to demonstrate how they could tell the human "was a fisherman, good-looking, was part of a small band of people (why not large band?), that his people moved about, that he lived in a simple sewn tent or mat hut, that he wore well-tailored clothes."[203] Deloria, in rare form, said the descriptions of Kennewick Man were purely "speculation, fantasy and hypothesis."

He then skewered the scientists' claims by declaring,

> to imply that these characteristics ... are the result of scientific work is ludicrous. They might as well add that they can prove the man was a Lutheran, an Elk, a member of the American Legion, that he lived with nearly a million people around him, was an expert fly-caster, and owned a clothing store where his employees used all those fine needles."[204]

In closing, Deloria wrapped up his taut legal and moral arguments by declaring that

> the "scientific case" for requiring the U.S. Army Corps to allow testing of these materials is shaky to non-existent. Scholarly opinion is overwhelmingly on the side of the proposition that "race" cannot be determined by scientific means. No evidence of one "wave of immigrants" let alone several is now possible, eliminating the various theories that have been put forth to distinguish modern Indians from their ancestral remains. The burden of proof is clearly on the plaintiff scientists to provide the U.S. Army Corps of Engineers with modern scientific theories that do not depend on outmoded 19th century concepts which are taken uncritically as proof.[205]

While the scientists scored early legal victories in their efforts to study the remains of Kennewick Man, eventually the tide turned and five Native nations—the Umatilla, Yakama, Colville, Wanapum, and Nez Perce—finally received word in 2015 that the corps had conceded the remains were, indeed, those of a Native individual and should be reburied under the rubric of NAGPRA.

In 2016, US senator Patty Murray and congressman Denny Heck, both of Washington State, sponsored legislation to expedite the repatriation, and the directive was ultimately passed as part of the Water Infrastructure Improvements Act for the Nation. Signed into law by President Barack Obama in December 2016, the act instructed the Army Corps of Engineers to begin the process for transfer of control back to the related tribes via the Washington State Department of Archaeology and Historic Preservation within ninety days of the signing date. The remains of the Ancient One were returned and appropriately and secretly reburied in February 2017.

Constitutional Reconciliation and the Revival of Treaties

Deloria's 1999 book cowritten with David E. Wilkins, *Tribes, Treaties, and Constitutional Tribulations*, entailed a comprehensive examination of the US Constitution's major clauses, doctrines, and amendments insofar as they apply or do not apply to Native nations and individuals. Deloria ended the study by reiterating a point he had been making since the 1960s—that the process of creating innovative diplomatic accords, also known as treaties, should be revived:

> It is long overdue that the federal government once again restrict itself to the exercise of the only clear traditional manner of dealing with Indian tribes—the treaty relationship. The commerce clause should be authority primarily for Congress to adjust the domestic law of the United States to conform to the obligations and responsibilities accruing to the government as a result of the treaties it makes with the Indian tribes, and the property clause should be authority primarily acknowledging the unique geopolitical nature of the tribes as preexisting sovereigns who live surrounded by states and the federal government, the latter-day sovereigns.[206]

In a wide-ranging 2000 interview with MariJo Moore representing *News From Indian Country*,[207] Deloria spoke assertively both about the positive gains Native peoples had made since the 1960s as well as the negative anti-Indian backlash that had resurfaced in response. During this interview, he made comments and gave suggestions for Native nations, which will be discussed in chapter 3, and also made two major recommendations for Congress.

First, he noted that the anti-Indian backlash (e.g., the sports mascot issue, Kennewick Man, environmental issues) had dramatically intensified in recent years and that state officials, who are constitutionally denied any direct role in Indian affairs, were, nevertheless, the parties most often leading the charge against Native economic and political gains and cultural developments.

Then Deloria observed that one of the reasons Tribal nations struggle in federal and state courts, particularly in treaty interpretation cases, is because Indigenous elders have long been denied status as "expert witnesses." Generally, only so-called academic experts, who tend to be non-Natives who have "studied" tribal nations, are accorded such status, thus denying the legitimacy of Native oral traditions and the knowledge that Natives are, or should be, the recognized experts of their own histories. The implication here is that Native peoples, the Congress, and the courts should work to rectify this denial of an Indigenous understanding of history. But since treaty interpretation cases are litigated in federal courts, and since Congress is the principal trust agent, the responsibility for addressing this injustice falls to the members of that body.

In a 2001 essay, Deloria returned to the issues of reconciliation, rehabilitation, consolidation, and repatriation.[208] He emphasized that Native nations, in order to fortify their political relationship to the United States, needed to muster a comprehensive plan detailing the economic, cultural, and political effects of various disastrous federal policies (e.g., removal, allotment, forced assimilation, termination) on their nations.

He used the Dawes Act of 1887 as an example of a failed policy that clearly violated the treaties and trust relationship. Since allotment had been empirically proven to have contributed mightily to the persistent poverty of the majority of Native allottees and their descendants, Deloria reasoned that tribal governments could assemble the data required to quantify the damage done over generations. This information could then be used as the basis for negotiations with Congress, with the goal of creating a rehabilitation act to help Native nations begin the road to economic recovery.

This would, if done properly, facilitate reconciliation between the two peoples and prove educational for all parties. As he astutely observed, "Both Indian and white people get a little tired of hearing 'well you broke the treaties.' That's obvious, so be specific—how did they break the treaties? And then go into the facts, that there was never a chance to escape poverty because of the way the Allotment Act was administered."[209]

This would be the first step in a fundamental process of intergovernmental reform. The next would be a comprehensive land consolidation plan in which Congress would enact a law returning to Indigenous peoples the power of land consolidation. Consolidated tribal lands would generate viable rural industries that would stabilize tribal economic security.[210]

Interestingly, eight years later, land consolidation would become one of the key elements in the culmination of the thirteen-year-long *Cobell* class action lawsuit, an endeavor that spanned three presidencies, resulted in seven trials, produced twenty-two published judicial opinions, and went before a federal appeals court ten times.

On December 8, 2009, the Obama administration announced that a $3.4 billion settlement had finally been reached with the significant aid of Congress, leading Native interest groups, and, of course, the Cobell legal team.[211] President Obama said, "With this announcement, we take an important step towards a sincere reconciliation between the trust beneficiaries [Native peoples] and the federal government and lay the foundation for more effective management of Indian trust assets in the future."[212]

The settlement contained three main components. It was initiated with the creation of a $1.4 billion account to be utilized for settlement of accounting and mismanagement claims. From this fund, each account holder was to receive approximately $1,000 for historical accounting claims. Then, a $100 million Trust Administration Adjustment Fund was established to increase the minimum payment made to members of the class.

Finally, a $1.9 billion Tribal Land Consolidation Fund was designed to be held and administered by the Interior Department with the intent of purchasing fractionated interests in trust or restricted lands from individual Indians on a voluntary basis. The agreed-upon terms directed that consolidated lands be turned over to tribal governments for purposes of reconsolidation. This fund was of particular importance for all of Indian Country since fractionation of individual allotments, which had resulted in thousands of undivided beneficial ownership interests, was, and continues to be, a major impediment to effective economic development, tribal jurisdiction, and trust administration.

The settlement also begat a five-member Secretarial Commission on Indian Trust tasked to provide recommendations for long-term trust reform. Ken Salazar, then secretary of interior, said in a statement to the Committee on Indian Affairs that "with this settlement we will turn the page on a dark chapter in Indian Country and begin to move forward, together toward our common goals."[213]

The final settlement was approved in July 2011 and incentive awards were made to the four original plaintiffs, led by Elouise Cobell who was to receive $2 million. James LaRose was granted $200,000, and Penny Cleghorn and Thomas Maulson were each to receive $150,000.

Appeals were filed by several individual Natives concerned about various aspects of the final settlement but, by the end of 2012, all appeals had been dismissed or withdrawn, with the appellate court stressing that the settlement was as fair as possible given the complexity of the case. On December 11, 2012, the district court formally approved the commencement of payments to Historical Accounting Class members, and distribution of checks to all living class members began the following week.

It is far too early to tell if the settlement act will ultimately lead to the fundamental reconciliation between the federal government and the several hundred thousand Individual Indian money account holders, as Deloria had hoped.

As with the Indian Claims Commission process (1946–1978), lawyers' fees consumed a large proportion of the award—nearly $99 million—while the average Native allottee and account holder netted only between $1,000 and $2,000. And since the BIA, the agency responsible for decades of tribal resource mismanagement, was kept in charge of overseeing the remaining trust resources and consolidated lands, there is legitimate skepticism as to whether this lengthy litigation/legislation truly culminated in genuine justice and greater security for Indian Country.

Remedies and Reckonings

In May 2001, a decade before the advent of fracking and other environmentally degrading methods of fossil fuel extraction that would later boost the economies of the Great Plains, Deloria returned to Rapid City, South Dakota at the request of the city's Chamber of Commerce to deliver a luncheon talk about population trends and cultural changes for both Natives and non-Natives. He pointed out that in South Dakota, projections showed that within the next decade 20 percent of the state's population would be over sixty-five years of age. He strongly suggested that the voters hold the state's politicians accountable to make sure the social security system remained solvent.

Deloria proposed a solution to address the potential economic downturn that would naturally result from an aging, dwindling population: reestablishment of the buffalo herds. He contended that white ranchers would learn from Natives how to properly treat animals and eventually develop a spiritual relationship with them that is unknown in the cattle industry. As he acerbically noted: "You can't really admire a cow, but you can admire a majestic buffalo."[214]

Today, grassroots organizations such as Dakota Rural Action, a coalition of small agriculture, ranching, and conservation groups, are actively concerned with questions of environmental degradation, population decline, and economic stagnation and are working to change long accepted, yet unsustainable, farming and ranching practices based on outmoded, nineteenth-century European models. Through efforts such as theirs, science and economics are finally catching up to millennia of Native experience and understanding of how to successfully live and thrive as part of the Great Plains ecosystem.

Deloria's next comment was aimed at tribal communities. He pointed out that no historic Indigenous nation north of the Rio Grande River ever governed more than 20,000 people, and that as Native nations' population had increased there was a need for more creative governing mechanisms. He advocated establishment of lower-level tribal governance entities such as townships that would be more effective in providing responsive leadership to communities.[215]

Deloria's final book, *The Legal Universe: Observations on the Foundations of American Law* (2011), coauthored with David E. Wilkins, is a richly detailed account of how Western law and social contract theory impact the rights, resources, and identities of numerous entities, including corporations, the natural world, children, women, and the four major racial/ethnic groups—African Americans, Latin Americans, Asian/Pacific Islander Americans, and Indigenous peoples.

Deloria had begun to give serious thought to these questions in the late 1980s. In fact, he suggested them to me in April 1987 as a possible term paper topic for a graduate seminar I was taking while a student at the University of North Carolina at Chapel Hill. At that time he said:

> In writing your paper you might raise the question that if the social contract theory is so good, why has American constitutional history featured a struggle by women and minorities to gain some 'standing' as legal persons within that contract? In other words, there can *never be* a neutral political theory that does not include gender and age and some preliminary acknowledgment that culture has a definite influence on the manner in which words and concepts are understood.[216]

To further his point he concluded that "even the packed Reagan [Supreme] court has now ruled in favor of women several times and it is supposed to be absolutely neutral in its interpretation of the Constitution. I would put that in a footnote because it does illustrate that even a determined effort by knotheads to change the interpretation of the Constitution to *favor* men has failed the test."[217]

In the first part of *The Legal Universe*, Deloria and Wilkins elaborate on the philosophical, historical, and political foundations of Western law and emphasize the dominant role that John Locke's articulation of *property*, as described in his understanding of the social contract, had on the Founding Fathers.

Locke's definition of property had two distinct meanings: one being the personal freedom and sovereignty that every person possesses because of their individuality, the other being "the material objects that humans create by mixing their labor with the raw materials of nature to produce something of value within a social context."[218] In other words, "Without property, a person has no standing; without a person, property has no meaning."[219] But as argued in the book, the property side of the social contract has long been denied to all those who are not rich white men.

The lack of political, legal, and property status of the various nonpolitical minorities—women, children, the LGBTQ community, people with disabilities, and the major racial and ethnic groups—has forced these groups "to develop some legal recognition and therefore constitutional protection for their personhood."[220] Even then the terms *citizen* and *person* have frequently been defined in ways that deny or belittle the rights of the members of nonpolitical minorities. Those who are members of more than one nonpolitical minority group, such as women of color and people of color with disabilities, have an even more difficult struggle.

The major recommendation that emerged in this study is that the federal courts should revive, expand, and strengthen Locke's first definition of property, which emphasizes the notion of personal freedom and personal sovereignty. "The real property of the social contract," according to the authors, "is the genius of human personality, the creative realm of possibilities existing in the minds of individuals, not the product of their labor."[221]

Deloria and Wilkins further assert that US constitutional law is slowly moving to embrace the view that property is a function of person and personality, something evidenced by ever-expanding copyright and trademark laws that apply to intellectual property. Thus, while the US Constitution's fathers—and I use that gender-specific term deliberately—generally believed property was physical, "subsequent experience indicates that the *most valuable* [emphasis theirs] property is human personality because it constantly creates new uses for nature."[222]

The most essential function of government, Deloria and Wilkins concluded, should be education: to create the institutions and conditions within which human personality can reach its full potential. Teachers at all levels, government officials from local, state, tribal, and the nation should be about devising opportunities and educational programs that would create conditions under which "the maximum number of minds and personalities can be developed most completely."[223]

From the mid-1960s to mid-2005, Deloria produced an incomparable body of data, including many recommendations, reforms, and remedies, in his relentless examination of the many facets of Indigenous political, legal, and cultural life—particularly as those aspects of life had been hampered or abused by the various branches and agencies of the federal and state governments. Also during this same period, and in many of these same writings, he was just as critical of Native nations and their political figures, cultural teachers, and scholars.

In chapter 3, we turn our attention to the suggestions and ideas Deloria proffered that might ameliorate many of the ongoing problems and tensions generated by and within Native nations themselves.

Chapter 3

FEET OF CLAY

Challenges, Ideas, and Admonitions to Native Governments and Peoples

Deloria long maintained that Indigenous nations constituted unique political, economic, and cultural national entities that, given adequate resources and respect, could function most effectively for their peoples. Further, he believed that fully functional, sovereign Native nations would, in turn, provide beneficial lessons to the larger society. This attitude was in evidence in 1965 when he gave testimony in his position as executive director of the NCAI during hearings on S.966, an early version of what would eventually become the Indian Civil Rights Act in 1968.

He then noted that while much attention had been paid to the influence of the Iroquois Confederacy and the Great Law of Peace in the political understandings of Benjamin Franklin, Thomas Jefferson, and George Washington, in actuality, "at nearly every point, social, economic, political and patriotic, American Indians can contribute their knowledge of cultural interaction and social concern that is needed today in this country."[224] As an example, Deloria described how Native kinship systems precluded the need for juvenile delinquency programs because children were able to rely upon large extended families.

He also scoffed at the notion that tribal governments were nothing more than "transitional" governments and that they and their citizens would eventually be fully assimilated into the American mainstream. While agreeing that Native nations were indeed in a state of transition, he concluded that they were transitioning "to a new form of social understanding which, if understood by older people, would help solve some of the pressing social problems of today."[225] Deloria understood then, what is now borne out by the scientific community and increasingly recognized by the larger society, that "tribes are not vestiges of the past, but laboratories of the future."[226]

In *Custer*, Deloria gave a more focused appraisal of what tribal nations and Native individuals needed to do to strengthen their internal and external sovereignty. One of his main concerns was the exploitation of Native peoples by academics and academic institutions. He advocated that Native governments adopt policies to clarify and structure what social scientists, particularly anthropologists and sociologists, would be allowed to research.

Intellectual and cultural exploitation were, and to a large degree remain, inherent in many academic interactions with Native peoples. Generations of scholars have furthered their careers with work based on data taken from Indigenous peoples.

While Native peoples frequently shared knowledge and experience, academics, while readily accepting these gifts, have rarely returned anything of lasting value to the tribes. Their published works often held little relevance for the sources of their academic successes—people they often believed headed inevitably toward extinction. Deloria was more sympathetic to Native scholars, whom he knew struggled to succeed against the odds in their institutions. Yet, he also saw that the majority lacked the time or incentive to remain genuinely connected and beholden to their communities. Given the dearth of guidance and support, he feared the majority would ultimately adopt the intellectual paradigms of the larger society to succeed.

Whatever its rationale, Deloria found this exploitative, salvage scholarship shoddy and maddening. He wanted Native communities to take control of their resources and require anthropologists and other academics to apply to the tribal governing body for permission to conduct research that implicated Native members or their resources.[227] More importantly, the researcher "would be given such permission only if he raised as a contribution to the tribal budget an amount of money equal to the amount he proposed to spend in his study."[228]

In a personal letter written in May 1969 to his friend Robert Lane, an anthropologist and husband to Barbara Lane, respected in Indian Country for her work with Northwest tribes fighting for fishing rights, Deloria put it this way: "I would suggest, and I am doing so to every Indian tribe I talk with, that we place either a tax or a bounty on anthropologists and sociologists—that way they could provide us with some income whereas now they only take and rarely give."[229]

This sensible requirement of researchers would be of benefit to all parties, and Native peoples would cease to be viewed merely as passive enclaves of data. Importantly, some Native governments and organizations such as the National Congress of American Indians (NCAI)[230] have implemented policies like those Deloria suggested. A number of American Indian and Native studies programs have forged direct links to reservation communities, and there are still many opportunities for partnerships. The challenge lies in balancing the research needs of the community with the financial concerns of the institutions. Too often tribes have contributed monetary and cultural resources only to be shut out of decision making or access to relevant research.

Already evidencing a passion for the law, yet devoted to a vision of a system rooted in Indigenous values and norms, Deloria encouraged Native judiciaries to look toward the development of "an Indian common law comparable to the early English common law."[231] This is a recommendation he would restate many times—one that would more comprehensively reflect the cultural distinctiveness of Native nations if it could be implemented on a wide scale across Indian Country. Some Native legal scholars[232] in the United States, Canada, New Zealand, and other countries are making headway on this recommendation.

Ever the pragmatist, Deloria also saw in the modern-day corporation a technical tool that he believed would embolden and quicken the Indigenous economic renaissance. "Indian tribes," he said, "have always had two internal strengths, which can also be seen in corporations: customs and clans."[233] He encouraged Native governments to "form themselves as housing authorities, development corporations, and training program supervisors," while continuing to act according to tribal values and norms.[234]

A number of Native nations have heeded this advice and now wield successful, nimble economic corporate entities, having been freed from the substantial political interference that used to dampen nations' ability to be economically adroit. See, for example, the Confederated Tribes of the Colville Reservation's Colville Tribal Federal Corporation (CTFC), which elects a sixteen-member board to oversee thirteen business enterprises that include gaming, retail, and recreation and tourism, among other projects. The corporation employs more than 800 individuals and generates an average of $120 million a year for the confederated nations.[235]

The Squaxin Island Tribe near Olympia, Washington, formed Island Enterprises, Inc. (IEI) in the 1990s to serve as the economic development entity for the nation. IEI has four stated goals: (1) to operate established businesses with an aggressive strategy to maximize potential profits while maintaining accountability to the nation; (2) to develop and acquire businesses that achieve "positive cash flows, reduce the dependence on gaming, and provide specific employment opportunities for Tribal Members"; (3) to work with members who need assistance starting businesses; and (4) to assist other tribally owned businesses through planning, accounting, and marketing.[236]

Recolonization: Nations United to Retake Lands, Power, and Ideas

Another major issue for Deloria and Indian Country was the corrosive bifurcation of urban versus reservation-based and eastern versus western-situated Indigenous communities. These long-standing feuds originated in the federal policies of removal, relocation, and termination, all of which led to and perpetuated poverty conditions on reservations.

Deloria pressed for the formation of Native coalitions that would unite these separate but related groups in a way that would bring some level of solidarity, thus forcing the BIA and other federal agencies to accept their obligations to all Native people, regardless of their geographic or jurisdictional domicile. He exhorted Native youth, particularly urban-based youth, to seek out and establish relations with reservation-based traditional people. One particularly brilliant idea he proposed "would concentrate its attention on the coordination among the non-reservation peoples and the reservation programs on a regional or area basis. In that way migrations to and from urban areas could be taken into account when planning reservation programs."[237]

Deloria also successfully predicted what he called the "recolonization" of Indian Country, with Natives gradually returning to and reclaiming their rightful places in their former homelands. He referred to a group of Cherokees who had returned to Tahlequah, Oklahoma, from southern California. Additionally, as the non-Indian population in the Great Plains states continued to dwindle, an increasing number of Native people were making their way back to their original homelands, continuing this "recolonization" movement. The success of numerous Native gambling operations has, of course facilitated some of these changes, but the movement had already begun even before the first bingo halls were established in the late 1980s.

Although Deloria could foresee a time when significant numbers of Natives would begin to return to their homelands, he understood that, for many, urban life was the new reality, and that something more needed to be done to address their distinctive social, legal, and economic needs. In March 1970, Deloria wrote Bufort Wayt, who then headed the Intercultural Program at Fort Lewis College in Durango, Colorado, and proposed a research course that he thought would be useful.

"Briefly," he said,

> the course I am talking about would be directed study and research into contemporary Indian movements by having students design and create a national Indian or-

ganization for urban Indians by completely researching existing conditions in the urban areas, visiting selected cities on field trips, compiling reports on existing conditions, publishing a newsletter and a number of reports, learning where the existing government funds are and how they are allocated between urban and reservation peoples, and development of a contemporary bibliography on Indian books, reports, publications, etc., that would be made available to tribes, urban Indian centers, etc.[238]

Deloria continued to show great interest in organizing urban Indians, and in July 1970 he accepted an offer from Eugene Crawford of the American Indian Center in Omaha, Nebraska, to devote sixty hours a month for six months to work on the West Coast and in the Midwest to reorganize the American Indian United (AIU) organization that would provide representation, support, and assistance for urban individuals who were being ill-served by the federal government, the National Congress of American Indians, or both.

He was convinced that this organization was needed because "the majority of Indian people are in cities not on reservations … [and] they have a great many social problems because in many instances they have been forced off their reservation lands into the urban areas without any education and training."[239]

Additional interests and ideas anteceded a brief surge of scholarship on urban Natives that would finally emerge in the late 1970s, as well as the birth of a national Indian organization—the National Urban Indian Council, which had a short life.[240] A number of more contemporary books have been produced in the 2000s[241] that address the status of Native individuals in key cities, but there remains a pressing need for the kind of national comparative research that Deloria called for in 1970.

Organizing across Indian Country

In fall of 1970, just after he was hired by the Western Washington University Ethnic Studies program, Deloria was invited to give a talk at Eastern Montana College. He declined the request, saying that all of his time was currently being devoted to teaching and to addressing the following problems: (1) pursuit of federal recognition for the Nooksack and Stillaguamish of Washington State, (2) return of the Iroquois wampum belts, (3) prevention of further dissolution of Klamath Nation's lands, (4) fighting the Canadian government's White Paper that threatened termination of Native rights, (5) assisting with the *United States v. Washington* fishing rights litigation, (6) involvement in another federal case involving taxation of Indian allotments, *Stevens v. Internal Revenue*, (7) assisting with the transfer of Fort Lawton to the small Native nations of western Washington, (8) the Ute termination case, and (9) the Tigua (Texas) claims case. He ended the letter expressing his deep annoyance at other so-called "leaders" who, he said, "do nothing but talk and never get anything done. So I have made up my mind to work on these problems until we get some solution to them."[242]

In December 1970, Deloria received a letter from Sylvie Brachet of France asking if he thought, with the recent publications of *Custer* and N. Scott Momaday's Pulitzer Prize–winning book, *House Made of Dawn*, that we were witnessing the emergence of a new American Indian literature. She also wondered if Deloria felt there was a "link" between his work and that of novelist Momaday. He replied that he saw no indication of an Indian literary renaissance, rather Indian writers like himself and Momaday were merely "a fad," and most Americans had no deep concern for what was actually happening to Native peoples.

Deloria then drew an interesting comparison between himself and Momaday:

> Scott's book is very well done in terms of illustrating the emotional ordeal that is undergone by Indians in American society. He is much more poetic than I but is not involved in social issues that currently affect the Indian legal status. Thus Scott is not as controversial and does

much better writing and his stuff is about how Indians feel. What I am doing is telling about the problems that face us and the forces at work that keep us in servitude.[243]

He concluded by emphasizing that he and Momaday wrote for entirely different reasons. "My writing," he said, "is done with political motivation to seek to induce social change. Scott's is much more involved in correctly outlining Indian values and moods to the reader." Deloria stressed that Momaday's writing would "endure for a long time," but he both underestimated his own work's staying power and overestimated Indian Country's readiness to act by declaring that "I would expect my writing to be totally out of date within three years of publication. I hope that conditions change—if not then writing has been a waste of time."[244]

In August 1971, Deloria responded to a young non-Native professor interested in teaching a course about Indigenous philosophy and religion. He was encouraging, yet realistic, and said that rather than focus solely on Native religions, the professor should use her time "combining philosophical viewpoints underlying Indian religious myths with expanding fields of ecology, etc., to present a new flexibility for understanding the rise of *powers* in religion."[245] Drawing upon the knowledge he had gleaned by living in the Northwest, Deloria gave, as an example, a story about the relationship that Native nations in that region have with salmon and why a holistic, integrated approach to the study of religion was necessary.

"The Indians of the northwest coast," he said,

used to have salmon ceremonies and their religion was based upon ecological factors, then superstitious in part, and with some insights. Now pollution is destroying the fish. Nitrogen poisoning on the Columbia has nearly wiped out the Columbia River salmon. It is not inconceivable that salmon ceremonies will once again be useful *but created by superstitious whites who, confused and misunderstanding what pollution has done, out of desperation revert to pure fantasy in their effort to get the salmon to return* [emphasis his].[246]

He closed his letter by offering an interesting short biography of himself, including a statement about where he stood in the current landscape: "Lest you get confused, my great-grandfather was one of the most famous medicine men in the tribe; my grandfather and father were Christian missionaries. I have a degree in theology but prefer practical politics and law. Anyway, I stand intellectually within the Sioux religious tradition but in day-to-day affairs am simply a modernized politician who has to solve today's problems where they occur and not by standing on a hill praying."[247]

In 1971, Deloria joined forces with the Southwest Intergroup Council, an organization based in Denver that worked with all major ethnic and racial groups. He became the executive director of the council in 1972. During his brief stint in the organization, at the request of the Teacher Leadership Program of the City University of New York, he produced a detailed curriculum outline titled "Problems and Issues Relating to American Indians." It was a bold, comprehensive, and detailed curriculum that illustrated the breadth and depth of his knowledge of Indigenous peoples and issues. (See appendix for the curriculum).

In two works published in 1971, *Utmost Good Faith* and "This Country Was a Lot Better Off When the Indians Were Running It," Deloria charged both traditional and younger, formally educated Natives with two tasks: the first was to craft a broad "philosophy of Indian affairs" to serve as an effective guide as Native nations contended with the massive changes confronting their peoples, and that Natives needed to arrive at a workable understanding of the nature and meaning of *tribalism*.

While concocting a definition for a well-known word might seem an easy task, he knew, given the contrasting and entrenched interests in Indian Country, that this would be the real challenge. The dynamic was manifested by ongoing conflicts between traditional people and members of the NCAI, each entrenched faction vying for the right to set the tone of the debate on how to define the very nature of tribalism.

Traditionally minded people wanted tribalism understood as an "organized band of Indians following customs with medicine men and chiefs dominating the policies of the tribe," while those aligned with NCAI viewed the term more as a "modern corporate structure attempting to compromise at least in part with modern white culture."[248] This tension has only magnified in recent years, especially since the advent of gaming and other types of economic development, yet it remains to be addressed whether Native nations are to begin to repair the ideological, economic, and cultural rifts that still typify internal Indian Country relations.

In an article written for *The Indian Historian* in 1972, Deloria made several recommendations for Native people that warrant attention. First, he suggested convening a comprehensive convention that would gather all the national Indian organizations together. He declared that "we must define exactly what a national Indian organization is, who it represents, what fields it works in, how it relates to other groups, and foreclose the continued spawning of new organizations every time we have a conference."[249]

Elaborating further on his ideas for organizational reform, he wrote a letter to Randolph Peters, then head of Stanford University's Native American Program. Peters had written Deloria to solicit his ideas for a major conference that would address the role of Indigenous interest groups. In his letter to Peters on September 7, 1972, Deloria suggested a number of important philosophical and practical points for him to consider as he launched the conference idea. He began by asking, "How can organizations establish their credibility as to who they actually represent? We have the NTCA [National Tribal Chairman's Association] and NCAI both claiming to represent tribal Indians. NCAI requires a tribal council resolution to join and NTCA only allows tribal chairmen to join. Which group represents reservation peoples?"[250]

He then raised the question, "How much does each group consider its role to be that of policy maker and which areas does it work in to establish new policies?" He described how the American Indian Movement utilized protests in an effort to generate new policies; the NTCA mostly worked directly with the BIA; the NCAI was essentially a lobbying interest group in Washington, D.C.; and the National Indian Youth Council had another agenda. Deloria queried: "Now, where are policies really made with respect to 1) education, 2) resources, 3) legislation, 4) administrative rule changes, 5) public relations and information? Which group, then, should do what in cooperation with whom?"[251]

He also raised the issue of organizational relevancy to the current political and educational systems. "Why must NCAI and NTCA have regional vice-presidents based on BIA area offices?... Why not organize on a state by state basis to parallel Senate and House structures[?] In educational groups do we need to represent areas of the country or institutions of concentrated Indian educational programs[?]"[252]

He went on to question the financial dimension of organizational life. "How many groups," he opined, "actually have any income besides government grants? What is the potential income for memberships in any area—individual, tribal organization, urban centers, etc. How is this money to be used?"[253]

And he contemplated which organization was best suited to conduct broader policy and history studies. "Who is responsible for reviewing American history and informing tribes of what happened to their lands, fishing rights, etc., in the past?" And "what organizations," he asked, "can respond to international events such as the killing of Brazilian Indians, etc.?"[254]

In closing he said,

> There are probably a number of other things that might be covered [during the conference] and probably you can add to these. What your conference should shoot at, if at all possible, would be to draw up fairly specific guidelines for Indian people to consider and advocate within organizations. Not everyone need work on policy, have scholarship programs, or advocate administrative changes. We still don't have a general fund for political action like contributions to candidates' campaigns, [or] ways to lobby specific candidates in primaries, etc.[255]

Deloria would ultimately come to the conclusion that Indigenous political labor could be more strategically divided through creation of a comprehensive intertribal organization with the viable groups of that time. The American Indian Movement might serve as the activist organization, the National Congress of American Indians, would be responsible for lobbying and oversight, the National Indian Youth Council could focus on the distinctive needs of Indian youth, and the National Tribal Chairman's Association would be tasked with interacting with the Bureau of Indian Affairs.[256] Such an omnibus Indigenous strategy never materialized, but the idea of organizing just such a body, as difficult as it would be given the proliferation of Native interest groups, is a sound one that bears revisiting.

On Native Education

Native education occupied a special place in Deloria's worldview, as he was keenly aware of the important role education plays in developing or hindering an individual's personal development. He wrote quite a bit on the subject,[257] although early in his career he had little interest because he said the subject of Indian education was "shrouded in the mists of uncertainty."[258]

Similar to his vision for political organizations, Deloria called for cooperation, consolidation, and specialization for Indian studies programs in universities and colleges. He noted in 1972 that "we don't need a full Indian program for every college that has a couple of Indian students."[259] It would be more appropriate, he believed, to "concentrate our students and our programs at a number of selected schools and drop the remainder of the programs."[260] He felt regionally based organization to be a better, more realistic approach to meeting the academic needs of Native students. Each major university in the Southeast, Northeast, Midwest, and Southwest would serve as a focal point for their particular area within Indian Country.

Deloria concluded his 1972 article with a series of concise, astute recommendations. He felt Natives needed to be much more judicious in how they worked with the mass media to avoid exploitation and reinforcement of negative stereotypes. As evidenced by the participants in the Standing Rock protests of 2016 through their organization, outreach, and messaging, these skills are being honed and utilized for the benefit of communities.

Along with a reduction and consolidation in the number of Native interest organizations, Deloria also saw a need for a corresponding reduction and consolidation in the number of academic conferences, which then, as now, consumed many dollars and often served merely as regurgitations of previous years' revised resolutions and recycled ideas, cloaked in the latest, inaccessible academic jargon.

This idea was threatening to some Native academics, many of whom organized and networked through these events. In times of scarce funding and grant dependency, these gatherings offer high-status venues for the ambitious to raise profiles and enhance résumés. Deloria knew that, at their best, conferences sustain Native scholars by allowing them safe spaces to share ideas and encouragement. At their worst, they are self-referential, ivory-tower oases removed from the critical needs of Indian Country. He opined that those most enthusiastic about conferences were usually the academically insecure who relied on pedantic displays to prove intellectual legitimacy. He was upset by the lack of useful and original scholarship as well as what he saw as the rapid erosion of oral presentation skills—sadly ironic for those with roots in oral traditions. This was the basis for his infamous scorn for the use of PowerPoint.

Finally, Deloria stated that Native nations should hire full-time lobbyists and have them in every state capitol, not just in Washington, D.C., to keep watch on state lawmakers and to improve tribal-state relations. Gaming tribes, in particular, have since taken heed of this advice and work regularly within their states to actively influence legislative agendas.

Clyde Warrior and the Poor People's Campaign

In October 1972, Deloria received a letter from a graduate student, Charles Heerman, of Oklahoma State University. Heerman was researching the Ponca Tribe of Oklahoma and, in particular, the role of Clyde Warrior, a noted Native activist, in the Poor

People's Campaign. He was interested in knowing more about Deloria's relationship with Warrior. Deloria, who usually responded
quickly to letters, did not write Heerman back until December 3,
1972. But his five-page, single-spaced, typewritten letter provides
real insight into his relationship with Warrior and how they each
approached the Poor People's Campaign and activism in general.

He commenced with a description of his own role with the
Poor People's Campaign, saying it "was directly based upon
Clyde's." He explained that he and Warrior "had been politi-
cal rivals and allies in the NCAI for a number of years" and that
Warrior had been the "major figure" responsible for getting him
elected to directorship of the NCAI.[261]

Deloria stressed he and Warrior, in their work at NCAI and
beyond, were attempting to "get Indians mad enough to fight for
their own rights but try to channel the anger into cultural renewal." "Clyde," he said, "was very traditional about Indian dancing,
customs, etc. One question we had which is not yet resolved is
whether or not Indian tribal customs could be revived to the point
where tribes could kick out the government and still hold lands
and communities intact."[262]

It was clear by the tone of the letter that Deloria had a great
deal of respect for Warrior as a thinker and political strategist.
"One thing I am fairly certain of," Deloria wrote, "Clyde was not a
media Indian like the current AIM people. He was always letting
Mel Thom, Bruce Wilkie and others get on radio and TV and
we would watch or listen to them and criticize their inability to
handle the questions for maximum media impact."[263]

While he and Warrior shared an aversion for the national
spotlight, Deloria noted they had disparate strategic approaches,
at least early on:

> I would say in conclusion, that I was highly sold on using
> legal-political channels—lawsuits, voter registration,
> etc., while Clyde was as highly sold on cultural renewal
> and reviving tribal customs, but neither of us depended
> or thought highly of simple media impact which was
> quite popular in those days. We both thought that the
> vague threat of a possible uprising floating around was

much more effective than direct confrontation.... I believe that we waged a very sophisticated psychological
warfare.[264]

Finally, in response to a question about Clyde's opinion of the
effectiveness of the Community Development Corporation (CDC)
in Indian Country, Deloria admitted that he had come to agree
with Warrior's position, and this would be a position for which he
would advocate for the rest of his life: "I have changed my mind
to Clyde's position. I would prefer cultural renewal to legal and
political change and when cultural customs are better entrenched
and there is the possibility of using them to control unscrupulous
Indian leaders then political change can be effective."[265]

A Critique of the American Indian Movement (AIM)

In 1973, Deloria stepped forth to challenge the tactics and strategies of some of the more activist-oriented Native organizations'
leadership that had played key roles in the Alcatraz Takeover,
Fort Lawton, Wounded Knee II, and the Trail of Broken Treaties. He emphasized that while the goals of land restoration and
treaty rights enforcement were certainly laudable, he believed that
there were two major problems with the way Native protests had
evolved to that point. The structure of many of the protests was
problematic. He stressed that the Indian activists had "failed to
pinpoint precisely the background of our oppression."[266]

In the same essay, Deloria also criticized the elected leadership
of some Native governments. He asserted that a number of elected
tribal officials had grabbed hold of the idea of tribal "self-determination" not to enrich their peoples' lives but rather to "increase
their own personal political power over tribal members and never
[allowing] a movement within the tribe of more democratically
based programs and ideas."[267]

In a lengthy 1973 *Indian Voice* interview with Laura Wittstock, Deloria elaborated further on issues he had with the strategies employed by AIM leaders.[268] He said,

> I think the whole AIM syndrome is to dramatize conditions. They do that pretty well, but once you dramatize the conditions and have gotten the people's attention, then you've got to have two or three times the energy and effort to put into convincing them you have a solution drawn up and your solution is better than anything they have ever thought about. That's my chief complaint with AIM. What they do is to come along and hit people over the head with a baseball bat, and the public turns and they say: "Ok, what's this?", and AIM says, "We're here to dramatize the conditions of Indians," and then they dramatize it three times longer than necessary, and keep raising all these issues as though they were all on the same level of importance. They may think that they are getting a settlement of issues, but one minor issue may be demanded as equally important as a very major issue. It really screws up their negotiations so they almost always end up negotiating amnesty for what they have already done. So where are you? You've muddied the water so much nobody in Congress can figure out what in the hell the Indians are on the warpath about. That's the main thing I find looking over this last year.[269]

He then analyzed the seventy-three-day-long Wounded Knee occupation and said that, in his estimation, a solution was evident by the second week: "It would have been worth it to have that protest if we only had two issues: a referendum on the tribal government and the [treaty] hearings on the Senate Foreign Relations Committee. If we could have narrowed all the things to those two points for the moment, and then arranged a date for the hearings, and started in on those hearings, then we would have had something."[270]

Deloria then noted that "if your only desire is to continue to dramatize—to symbolize our problems—by the end you haven't really accomplished anything. This is the big fallacy of Alcatraz. Indians realized it symbolized a new era of trying to get lands returned in the treaties upheld, but the symbol is only viable during the initial week or so of the protest. At that point it has to be *somehow* [emphasis his] translated into some kind of irreversible gains or concessions on the part of the government." Wittstock then asked, "What you are saying here then is that what you are quoted as saying in *Red Power* is that "symbolic action gets symbolic reaction?" Deloria concurred and said, "Yes, you said it better than I did."[271]

The events at Wounded Knee are of legendary importance and inspire many more than forty years later. However, to simply romanticize personalities and fail to scrutinize the actions taken is to show we learned nothing about wielding power. It is important to be inspired by resolve and yet still learn from the mistakes. Deloria's line of reasoning makes sense, as he was deeply influenced by another pivotal fight for treaty rights, the Pacific Northwest Fishing Wars, where in the 1960s and early 1970s tribes united to fight against the state of Washington to regain and protect their treaty-given subsistence rights.

Deloria's lifelong friends Billy Frank Jr. and Hank Adams were key leaders in this effort. Their message and tactics were simple and relentless. They maintained they were entitled to fish by the terms of the treaties negotiated in 1854 and 1855 with the United States. Guided by Hank Adams, who also magnificently assisted at Wounded Knee, they used creative nonviolent tactics and messaging, including recruitment of celebrities like Marlon Brando and Dick Gregory to their cause. Although arrested countless times and subjected to acts of violence, they budged neither from their message nor their goal. The result was the 1974 *Boldt* decision, acknowledging their treaty rights—a profound and lasting victory for both treaty rights and sovereignty.

The tactics used by the leaders of the 2016 Standing Rock encampment near the Standing Rock Reservation in North Dakota were similar to those used in the Fish Wars. Tribal nations and their allies at the encampment were focused on simple but profound goals—the protection of water, sacred sites, and land as part of treaty rights.

While Deloria agreed with AIM's major objectives of having Indian treaties upheld, resolving the status of urban Indians and supporting self-determination for all Native peoples, he said he would have added another issue: "I think the most important current objective is to try to pull the various Indian communities together in terms of establishing a contemporary identity with each other. This would create a different feeling in each community out of which people can act as representatives of that community." Projecting ahead ten years, besides the need for an expanded land base, he stressed that tribal governments had not been as effective as they needed to be. "They have only acted defensively," he said, "and haven't gone out and proposed something positive. Saying, for example, we are going back to having traditional government is really meaningless unless you are able to go and articulate how that is going to produce better conditions for individual communities."[272]

Finally, he urged Native leaders to be more precise in their complaints to the federal government about the problems bedeviling their peoples. Ever focused on the integrity of treaties, he said that,

> what you need to do is to have the individual tribes *authorize* [emphasis his] a study of their treaties and find out what they think are the current violations. Then send tribal representatives in to talk to individual congressmen and hand them written reports, say, "this is the text of our treaty and these are what we feel are violations, and we'd like a hearing in Congress and establishment of a new law identifying the particular rights we have against the states and against the federal government," and really clarify the situation.[273]

"If enough tribal nations did that," he continued, "that would have forced the Department of Interior to at least hold formal hearings on whether or not we could have extensive congressional hearings on treaties. This way you get those men on the record."[274]

In keeping with this controversial, challenging tone, in an article titled "The Next Three Years," written in 1974, Deloria noted that Natives had just entered a period of what he termed "Indian resurrection," and speculated how the future generations would judge the present generation of Indigenous leaders. He reasoned they might ask why the job of unification on various levels had not been achieved. And, they would wonder why the large western Native nations had been unwilling to assist the small eastern and northern communities. Finally, despite the progress made in reviving Native culture with its emphasis on "sharing," would they be bewildered by the fact that some Native peoples "refused to share their fate with the other tribes, and the whole Indian revival dispersed with each tribe attempting to go it alone, a strategy that had previously proved disastrous on many occasions?"[275]

He concluded the piece by declaring Native peoples needed to force the federal government to reconsider those laws, rules, and regulations that had long oppressed them. "We are at the stage," he insisted, "where we must force the government to clarify its policies, to streamline its programs and to deal honestly with all Indian communities, large and small, eastern and western, urban and rural."[276]

In "Religion and Revolution Among American Indians" (1974), Deloria again focused his attention on the rising tension within Native communities between those individuals who had generally assimilated into the American body politic and could thus be easily classed as ethnically Native but middle-class Americans, and the so-called Native traditionalists, who generally adhered to different values, seeking to retain, and act from, an Indigenous worldview.

While evincing great respect for the traditionalists, Deloria also called upon them to acknowledge that "the basis of Indian tribal religion is not preserving social forms and ceremonies but creating new forms and ceremonies to confront new situations."[277] This view, he held, was pivotal, given that Native customs and beliefs are shaped by particular times and places. In order to be meaningful, religious traditions must "relate to a dramatically changed community in a dramatically changed environment."[278] He considered that traditional people should understand this intuitively, since tribal religions are not dependent upon the teachings of saviors and because truth manifests "in the ever changing experiences of the community."[279]

In closing, Deloria reflected his core positive belief in the inherent sovereignty of each Indigenous community: "The shape of the Indian future cannot be imported, either from Washington or from other struggles for social change."[280] Here, once again, he asked the major, elemental question, "*What shall be the true and accepted meaning of the tribe?*" While it was at that time conceptualized as a "quasi-political entity," some wanted it to also encompass the concept of economic viability. For Deloria, however, the hope was that "the tribe" might once again become identified at its core as "a religious community."[281]

On the Life-Sustaining Need for Traditional Education

While Deloria always emphasized the primacy of "the tribe" as a natural entity with many facets, he also expressed support for the autonomy and personal rights of talented Native individuals to forge their own paths in their efforts to cope with the rapid flux of cultural transformation. He observed that these are the individuals often criticized and ridiculed by tribal members if they attempt to break into fields considered removed from Native life, whether that be in small business, professional careers, or even folk singing.

Envisioning these individuals almost as cultural liaisons, Deloria noted that "if Indians are to survive the rapid cultural change that the rest of society is making, the Indian community will simply have to allow some of its members to develop their talents and contacts with the rest of American society."[282] This continues to be an issue in Indian Country, although it appears to have lessened in intensity somewhat, given the larger and increasingly diversified Indigenous population. The pendulum seems to have since swung the other way, as now while those trained to be successful outside tribal communities are more accepted, they often find rewards elsewhere.

When Deloria asserted that the three areas most likely to have a direct impact on the future of Native nations were higher education, Indian culture, and Indian control of educational institutions,[283] he provided a number of suggestions on the types of studies academic and nonacademic individuals should undertake that would be of tangible benefit to tribal nations. Native nations should start, he contended, by closely examining the many controversies their communities had faced during the past several centuries, and, importantly, they should commence by drawing upon, as a principal source of firsthand information, the oral recollections of living tribal members.

As an example, Deloria suggested that the Pueblos, rather than continued fixation upon the exploits of Spanish conquistador Coronado and the Great Pueblo Revolt of 1680, should instead "be doing extensive writing and interviews of the elder Pueblo people concerning how they organized and eventually won the battle for their lands in 1924."[284] Other tribal researchers and Native academics should similarly focus on contemporary events that had profound effects on the historical and contemporary status of tribal nations.

He also proposed the idea of extended seminars, a year or so in duration, that would bring together Natives and allies to discuss a variety of topics such as literature, art, history, and ethnoscience. Despite the basic informality of tribal social systems, Deloria noted that "we really don't have an informal network of Indian writers like dissident groups of whites have. Each writer is writing in isolation."[285] Importantly, he suggested that such extended gatherings should have an aspect of informality and interdisciplinarity about them so that substance rather than theory or jargon would hold sway, and people would be interested in one another as individuals and not as followers of a particular discipline.

In 1974, Deloria published *Behind the Trail of Broken Treaties: An Indian Declaration of Independence*. Unlike most of his other books, this study was inherently collaborative and featured the work of several other writers, including Kirke Kickingbird. In it,

Deloria and other writers mustered a number of arguments as to why Indigenous people deserved international recognition.

Treaties, as principal sources of laws recognizing the political nationhood of Native nations were viewed as essential elements in such recognition. Treaty-making processes at both the domestic and international levels were analyzed.

The Twenty Point Proposal penned largely by Hank Adams and others during the Trail of Broken Treaties Caravan across the United States in 1973 had raised the idea of US Senate Foreign Relation Committee hearings on treaties. Deloria and several other Native lawyers had approached the committee about holding such hearings, and progress was made until some of the more radical AIM members gave rogue speeches in New York City. Their fiery rhetoric upset Senator J. William Fulbright, who then put a halt to the proposed hearings.

Frustrated with the lack of domestic solidarity and unified purpose, Deloria declared in a May 1973 letter that "I have switched somewhat to a more international posture on aboriginal peoples and lands and have been working with some of the anthropologists at the Smithsonian Institution."[286]

Casting Off the Colonial Yoke of Wardship

By the late 1970s, fervid Indigenous activism began to wane, ground down by a variety of forces, including federal harassment and infiltration, imprisonment of Native leaders, or the energy simply being channeled in other directions. Deloria posited that while there had been a number of developments arising out of the maelstrom period of the 1960s and 1970s, "The missing ingredient in the formula for constructive change was a unified Indian community capable of articulating and interpreting future goals."[287] Thus, Indian Country had been unable to arrive at a "theoretical conception of the contemporary status of Indians," leaving Native America essentially rudderless and subject to being cast "to and fro between the twin poles of sovereignty and wardship."[288]

In written testimony to the Subcommittee on Elementary, Secondary, and Vocational Education of the Committee on Education and Labor, Deloria argued in 1980 that both Native peoples and Congress needed to work on returning control of education to local communities. He saw that the key to educational success for Native children was inclusion of the content and substance of Indigenous traditions as a way to make the educational process more meaningful to Native students. As he described it:

> In practical terms this type of education would reduce the administrative role to an absolute minimum in favor of a greatly expanded teaching staff dealing with an increasingly small class of students on increasingly specific subjects of instruction. The traditional Indian teaching format approaches the tutorial in its specificity enabling both student and teacher to share a particular learning-teaching activity and dealing specifically with the knowledge and experiences of the world in which the teacher has lived and in which the student expects to live. The content of this kind of education emphasizes how to live in the world and what it means to be a human personality within a social-political context.[289]

He reminded the committee that Native student test scores decline and dropout rates increase around the time of adolescence and told them that historically tribal ceremonies had helped young people cope with that confusing period of life. He urged that these tribal ceremonies be "made a regular part of the educational experience even if it means that children of this age will not formally attend school for a year while they are instructed in traditional customs and beliefs and made an adult part of the community."[290] If these ceremonies were to be incorporated, Deloria judged that many of the most significant problems facing reservation communities, such as spiraling crime rates, gang activity, alcohol- and drug-related problems, and teen suicides would be addressed and resolved in a manner that comported with Indigenous values and traditions.

The public incorporation of Native history and culture would not be seriously undertaken for another twenty-five years, when state lawmaker John McCoy (Washington/Tulalip) sponsored a bill adding these topics to the Washington State public schools curriculum in 2005. Even this relatively modest acknowledgment of the existence and contributions of Native peoples took several years to become law. Now known as "Since Time Immemorial," it was formally instituted in 2015 by the Washington State legislature via SB 5433. This curriculum has become a model for other educational proposals introduced across the country.

Vital Native Cultures, Rooted in Traditional Values

While he had many criticisms and suggestions for Native activists, Deloria saved some of his more biting critiques for tribal officials, both elected and appointed, who by the early 1970s had come to constitute what Philip S. Deloria once called a "managerial class" of Native elites.[291] Many of these individuals established cozy relationships with federal officials administering the Great Society and War on Poverty programs. They became adept at gaining access to external funding sources and used that power to secure tribal offices and/or leadership positions within national Indian organizations.

As Deloria noted, "The Indian relationship to the federal government changed significantly as [federal] programs increased. Access to the federal government was restricted by the vision of professional Indians and their conception of what was programmatically possible to obtain.... Indian leadership was inclined to take programs that could be easily funded rather than programs where the needs were the greatest."[292]

Such a process proved especially debilitating to those tribal traditions and institutions centered on leadership. "Reservation people," Deloria argued, "were not inclined to use traditional mechanisms for approval or disapproval of their leaders because the criterion that quickly developed was whether or not the person could obtain federal funds, not his or her trustworthiness in view of the larger social and cultural goals of the community."[293]

Unless this pattern of economic and political relations between the managerial class of Natives and federal agencies was changed, he foresaw few permanent solutions to Native problems. The system was, in Deloria's words, "self-sustaining so long as it can maintain the facade of representing the community which has become its clientele." Therefore, "since funds are forthcoming only to meet the continued needs of the reservation community, it is to the advantage of the pyramidal tract of professional workers to ensure that no real solutions are forthcoming, since the resolution of any problem would only produce a reduction in funds, opportunities, and the institution itself."[294]

Deloria recognized this self-defeating pattern in another 1982 essay, "Education and Imperialism," where he once again called for a curriculum grounded in Indigenous values. He was deeply concerned that too many Native education conferences were focused on discussing "rules, regulations, and waivers" and how to get refunded rather than on the actual education of Indigenous children.[295]

Thus, he proposed developing "an educational program which enables Indians to understand fully their own cultural roots and to have increasing reliance on the usefulness and rationality of tribal customs."[296] Ever aware that Native peoples live in a complex and differentiated modern society, he also declared that along with the tradition-based program there "must be a general humanistic-liberal arts-social science complex whereby Indians can learn the most important general ideas which underlay specific institutions in American life."[297]

Realizing that such a program could not be instantly adopted, given that most Natives had attended Western-based systems and would need a certain amount of "deprogramming," he proposed a workable compromise that would "introduce new programs during the transitional phases of the present educational experience," so that, "between grade school and high school, between high school and college, and between undergraduate and graduate school, Indians should have available to them a special year during which they can stabilize the cultural/religious/social/philo-sophical changes they are experiencing."[298]

For example, in this holistic, community-based approach to education, a young person at the end of their grade school years, and with puberty and adolescence just beginning, would be sent to live with tribal elders of their own gender in order to learn Indigenous customs and knowledge, to participate in puberty ceremonies, and to generally receive the help needed to make the difficult transition from child to young adult. A similar transitional period would be granted to graduating high school students and college students as well.

Deloria suggested that each of these transitional years were critical for two specific purposes: first, to provide an important pause in the necessary process of learning about non-Indian society "in which the student could reaffirm the traditional basis of his or her own society and gain personal confidence which would enable him or her to proceed to the next step in the educational process"; and second, "it would give the student an opportunity to improve their basic reading, writing, and research skills so they would be better equipped to handle the demands of schooling on the next level."[299]

In yet another 1982 article, "American Indians: Landmarks on the Trail Head," Deloria proposed an area of research that is still desperately needed: a national study of Native voting patterns.[300] For such a critical issue, there is still very little data on this subject, despite the fact that Natives received the franchise via a federal law in 1924 (although many had attained it previously via treaties and specific statutes), and despite the amount of attention that has been devoted by historians and anthropologists to assess the degree to which Native peoples have assimilated in American society. More serious attention has been given to the matter of late. In the wake of the current Native gaming phenomenon, Indian voting patterns have changed dramatically, with many more Natives voting in state and federal elections, and there is an increasing body of literature on the topic.[301]

In 1983, Deloria coauthored *American Indians, American Justice* with Clifford M. Lytle, an important study of Native judicial systems. While stressing that tribal courts were doing vital work amidst a sea of financial, cultural, state, and federal constraints, the pair also strongly suggested that Native judiciaries and their committed jurists should be careful about the wholesale adoption or mimicking of state or federal laws and procedures.

They strongly advised that even if such Western institutions "must be adopted," they should be incorporated "in such a manner that they do not destroy the traditional components and familiarities of Indian law that still linger in a vulnerable condition. Adoption of these procedural formalities must not be allowed to intrude upon and dominate the informality of tribal courts, which reassures tribal members that the judge continues to work with the old traditions of solving problems rather than seeking retribution."[302]

In 1984, Deloria and Lytle continued their successful partnership with a much lauded critique of John Collier and the IRA, *The Nations Within*. A sterling policy analysis, this book also contained a bounty of recommendations.

They based their observations on the depiction of Indian Country as separated into two major categories of people: *traditional* or *tribal* people and *ethnic Indians*. While the members of both groups clamor for self-determination for their nations, they represent in some sense different visions of the world they inhabit, or aspire to inhabit. While these are ideal type concepts, since many Natives go back and forth between the two, there are still substantial differences between those who self-identify as belonging to one or the other camp.

One fundamental difference, the authors assert, is that "tribal peoples tend to vest entirely too much trust in the ability of American institutions to perform the moral acts that would be necessary to secure what they want. Ethnic Indians regard the tribal Indians as an unrealistic and overly romantic group that looks backward to old days and glories, not forward to new programs and experiences."[303] Tribal peoples often regard their ideological opponents as wholly without principles, pragmatic to the point of having no moral stance at all, and claim they regard the tribal government, not the people, as the tribe. In other words, tribal people support *idealism*, whereas ethnic Indians support *realism*.

The groups also diverge on their perceptions of the United States. Traditional people understand that the United States is simply one of many nations and that it, too, is bound by what transpires in the world. Their understanding of their own nation-hood imagines a time when they will join the family of nations as relative equals. Ethnic Indians, on the other hand, are more comfortable operating as one of many ethnic groups in the nation, albeit as unique groups.

These individuals, including most Native elected officials, "see the solution to this problem [shrinking land bases, exploited resources] in getting involved in American domestic politics, in litigation, legislation, and other forms of political action to ensure that the laws of the United States will be applied to the reserva-tions in the least harmful manner."[304]

Traditionally minded individuals, according to Deloria and Lytle, were concerned with the "substance of life," whereas ethnic Natives appeared more interested "in the process." The latter con-tended that something must be done to enable cooperation and communication for true, sustained progress.

With the establishment of this foundational paradigm, De-loria and Lyle moved into their specific recommendations. They recognized a need for many Native nations to structurally reform their governing institutions, but in a way that supported a strong linkage between traditions and contemporary times. They strong-ly called for what they termed "lasting cultural renewal" that would enable Natives to reconcile cultural identity in a contem-porary America. They also saw the necessity for Native nations to achieve economic stability, and finally, they encouraged more amicable relations between tribal nations, the states, and federal government.

Structural Reforms

- Increase the size of tribal councils to make them more representative and less subject to BIA intimidation.

- Establish a national governing body for Indigenous nations (a Native United Nations).

- Incorporate traditional customs like reconciliation and restitution in tribal court proceedings.

- Establish Courts of Elders to help resolve certain domestic and other internal disputes.

- Redefine the role of Native police officers and law enforcement policies to include peacemaking skills and direction.

- Allow the national governing body to charter tribal subsidiary groups.

Cultural Renewal

- Preserve and strengthen Indigenous languages.

- Utilize traditional foods and medicines to improve health.

- Treat cultural integrity as an essential force: Natives must define and enforce what is acceptable behavior and stop prostituting their cultural traditions and ceremonies for tourists and Western religious institutions.

Economic Stability

- Halt practices and policies that result in land loss; consolidate fragmented tribal lands.

- Utilize natural economies that do not cause ecological damage (e.g., aquaculture, fishing, berry picking, buffalo ranching, farming, and gathering methods that incorporate traditional knowledge and stewardship of resources).

Federal/State Relations

- Support treaty rights.

- Pursue full faith and credit relations with states.

- Engage in cross-deputization arrangements to improve law enforcement procedures.[305]

Deloria, for his part, was particularly adamant about the need for substantial structural reform of Native governments that more accurately reflected Indigenous values and traditions. In July 1987, he wrote me and said that "the proper way to revise tribal governments is to return to forms and structures that are as close to what the people once had as is humanly possible." He noted that such changes were already beginning to happen on the Pine Ridge Reservation in South Dakota where the Lakota were attempting to "create something like the old national council with the four shirt wearers and the elders having an important voice in decisions again."[306]

And he once again offered me a potential dissertation topic: an examination of traditional Dine (Navajo) governing systems. As he put it, I should think about "writing a dissertation on the traditional Navajo organization and how effective it would be in modern times." And he said if I chose this avenue I needed to "emphasize the religious nature of community leadership because I think that's where a lot of the answers are to be found."[307]

A Father's Passing, a Family's Legacy

Themes of religion and theology pervaded many of Deloria's works. In "Out of Chaos," written in 1985, Deloria turned his keen gaze to these topics and noted that, while colonialism had caused and was continuing to generate massive physical, psychological, and spiritual damage to Native peoples, it was still possible for Natives to turn this around and to recover their identities. Natives needed, he said, "to develop a new interpretation of their religious traditions with a universal application."[308] Moreover, tribal peoples should "seek out areas in which they could communicate with sympathetic people in the larger society, and put their own house in order."[309]

While admitting how difficult this would be, given rampant American hypermaterialism and the fact that many Natives had come to adopt the perception of the world as a basically physical thing, he nonetheless maintained that "American Indians contain the last best hope for spiritual renewal in a world dominated by material considerations."[310] We see a glimmer of this hope manifested by those who stand to protect their homes and the environment from more damage from destructive mining, oil carrying pipelines, valuing water over oil, life over money.

In March 1990, Deloria wrote me to say that the University of Colorado, urged on by his good friend, Norbert Hill, was making a serious push to hire him. Having lived in Colorado before his move to Tucson, he was open to their offer and later that year accepted a tenured position in Boulder that linked him to several colleges and departments—the Law School; the Departments of Religious Studies, Political Science, and History; and the Center for the Study of Race and Ethnicity.

These professional changes came at a dark time for him personally, as in that same month his father, Vine Deloria Sr., passed away. Deloria Sr. was a respected elder of the Standing Rock Sioux Nation and an eminent Episcopal priest who served that church for nearly sixty years. The Standing Rock Sioux sent the Delorias a kind letter of condolence, but Vine was deeply aggrieved by the failure of the Episcopal Church to acknowledge his father's death—so much so that in his letter to me he made an astounding revelation, "Now that [my father's gone] I can publicly support and recruit for the old traditional way. I didn't when he was alive because it would have embarrassed him."[311]

A week later, he wrote me a follow-up letter in which he described some strange issues he had had a few years earlier while trying to write an essay about the Vision Quest ceremony among the Lakota people. He said that for two consecutive summers he had been stopped cold by a series of strange events while preparing the manuscript:

> The first summer I reached page 206 and suddenly I had car trouble like you would never believe. One day three—count them—three—batteries on my cars went dead within half an hour. I had to wait at home for my son to get off work and then have him go to Sears and get new ones. Then my daughter … got in a car accident.

Then I bought a used car which gave me fits and never did work. Then I had to borrow all kinds of money to make it through the summer so my writing halted July 8th. The next year I was writing and reached page 207— on July 8th—and my mother got sick, my wife's mother fell down the stairs, I had to fly my mother down here and then fly to South Dakota and pack their things and move them down here. So that was the summer.[312]

Deloria went on to describe the piece on the Vision Quest ceremony he had attempted to write. He said,

It was to be about various quests that people had told about and an analysis of what it really meant to have a vision—not this New Age bullshit about power panthers and spiritual warriors and so forth. But I never had a strong beginning to it and am more or less back to some of the questions. It now occurs to me that I should tell the whole story of my family, from the old medicine men through two Episcopal priests and how when my family really needed the Episcopal Church it was nowhere to be found. And I am going to end the chapter by publicly stating that I and my family are now going to support and practice the old ways and forsake Christianity.[313]

It is important to understand the depth of pain and struggle that would have been involved in these thoughts. Deloria was a member of a family long interested in spiritual matters. His great-grandfather, Saswe, was a renowned medicine man who had a vision that directed the next three generations of Delorias to study both Christianity and Indigenous religious traditions. Deloria had long been attuned to matters of the spirit and heart, always believing that Indigenous spiritual knowledge and properly conducted ceremonies were keys to the strength and vitality of Native nations.

While there were a few other instances when he shared his intention of publicly disavowing Christianity and actively promoting traditional spirituality, I am unaware if he ever did so. While he always fiercely supported traditional ways, I am not sure what his relationship was with Christianity near the end of his life. I share this observation in order to show the deep complexity and sincerity of Deloria's thinking. He has deservedly become an iconic figure, but let us not forget his humanity as he struggled to pursue an honorable path for himself, his family, his community and, ultimately, for the world.

Western Science and Native Knowledge

In 1991, Deloria published *Indian Education in America: Eight Essays*, a series of articles he had previously written for *Winds of Change*, a publication of the American Indian Science and Engineering Society.[314] It was a comprehensive overview, analysis, critique, and prescription about education, ranging from traditional-based systems of knowledge to the flawed efforts of the federal government to transform tribal societies through Western education. The essays contain a number of recommendations for Native students and educators that bear attention. The work was so popular that it was revised and expanded in 2001 when Deloria's essays were joined with chapters by Daniel Wildcat in a book titled, *Power and Place: Indian Education in America*.[315]

In the pages of the 1991 study, we find Deloria once again urging Native students, particularly those who study science and engineering, to first gain or regain a solid understanding of their own nation's traditional knowledge about their families, ceremonies, lands and resources, and cosmology. He also recommended that Indigenous academics and those with professional expertise in other areas take the time "to offer their tribes predictive scenarios based upon their professional training. The degree to which an Indian professional can succeed with any tribal program will be measured by the number of possible scenarios with which he or she presents the tribe. It will then be the task of the tribe to choose among possible competing scenarios."[316]

Essentially, said Deloria, Native students and Native faculty, once they had acquired their formal training, would perform the same role that scouts did in the past. Scouts provided critical and detailed information to their communities and leadership, equipping them with the knowledge necessary to make appropriate decisions within the context of the group's values, goals, and traditions.

From his perspective, Indigenous students and teachers, in addition to learning from their own disciplinary training, must always be cognizant of the ways their educational experiences affect the preservation and sustained use of their tribal nations' lands and the effect of their educational training on their nations' ongoing existence.[317]

Finally, Deloria reiterated two fundamental subjects, the mastery of which he had long championed as essential for anyone who wished to be a truly educated Indigenous person: family genealogies and tribal traditions. These two subjects should be taught to all Native youth and the knowledge would, he maintained, "provide a solid foundation for children's personal identity as well as serving as a context for teaching all manner of social skills and development of memory and recollection. In a world of large institutional restraints, knowledge of family and tribe would provide a significant set of skills to provide confidence in the child that he or she is part of an ongoing human experience."[318] Deloria emphasized that these teachings should occur in the community and not in the school. This was important in keeping children connected to their families and communities.

More Ivory Than Red:
False Allegiances in Academia

In May 1992, as I was settling into my role as an academic at the University of Arizona and preparing to revise my dissertation for submission as a book, I wrote Deloria seeking his counsel on the best prose style to use. In his typical, frank style, he made several useful suggestions and then commenced to opine on the tone I should take.

He said,

> Don't include lower court cases—what you want to say is that if the whole court system is supposed to guarantee Indian tribes justice, why does the Supreme Court avoid meting out justice by inventing squirrely terms and logic in order to rule against the Indians? I would concentrate on the anti-Indian bizarre cases and not mention the beneficial cases. You have to get out into the public arena as an Indian advocate and not simply as a detached scholar. You want to force the issue of justice and fairness. If you present both sides of the issue of fairness people will simply say, let it all balance out over the years and stop bitching. You don't want that. Since a lot of people will not go to the trouble of looking at the beneficial side, your book will carry on the task of showing government oppression and suppression. That is what will enable you to become a leader for the next generation. We already have too many people being impartial.[319]

In 1995, Deloria authored a short essay titled "Rethinking Tribal Sovereignty," in which he unequivocally stated that Native governments could only claim to exercise internal sovereignty if they found a way to revive and reinstitute the majority of their social traditions. He noted as examples traditional methods of child adoption and utilization of reconciliation rather than restitution in resolving conflicts. He also suggested that tribal nations consider the possibility of installing a two-level form of government, "with a Council of Elders dealing with internal sovereignty issues and community topics, and the elected tribal or business council being in charge of conducting external sovereign affairs."[320]

In April of 1997 as I was finishing a first draft of my *American Indian Politics* book, I had occasion to write Deloria and seek his counsel. I was struggling to develop a simple graphic that would clearly depict the intergovernmental relationship between Native nations and the federal government. I had used the phrase "aboriginal sovereignty" to identify the origin point of that crucial, inherent power, but I wanted his view on the origins of that sovereignty and whether it resided in the people or in Indigenous governing systems.

He responded in a letter on April 22: "Well, the old timers at Pine Ridge [Reservation] used to tell me, when I was a tender lad, that they still retained sovereignty—that the tribal government was only a limited powers government and that the people reserved everything for themselves. I have followed that line of thinking ever since."[321] He continued by noting that "if the tribal government completely breaks down, the BIA calls a General Council meeting and has the people elect officers and adopt a new constitution, so that's got to make aboriginal sovereignty a mysterious but always useful thing."[322]

In 1998, Deloria trained his attention on Indigenous intellectuals and challenged them to utilize their talents and time anticipating and analyzing the multitude of problems adversely affecting tribal nations rather than simply discussing and redefining, in the halls of academe, certain concepts like hegemony, colonialism, self-determination, and sovereignty. He contended that mere discussion of these terms "assist us in creating a set of artificial problems, wholly abstract in nature, that we can discuss endlessly without having to actually do something."[323]

In typically blunt language, Deloria stated:

> I have great sympathy with Indians beginning their careers in academia and the desire, altogether human, not to get in trouble with white professors in their departments before they get tenure. No one expects them to rush into heated political situations and be branded militants or malcontents. But many Indians are so subservient that they have virtually no identity at all. Between their personal crises and academic meetings they could be producing a mass of literature that would help articulate the Indian position on many issues, and this kind of production would eventually influence how decisions

are made and how Indians are treated. Liberal arts and
social sciences are ripe for picking by anyone with critical faculties. Yet, the battles against derogatory images of
Indians, improper histories of tribes, and misinforma-
tion on tribal programs are still being carried on largely
by local Indian leaders, not by Indian academics.[324]

In short, Deloria was bemoaning the fact that a substantial
number of Native academics appeared to have a stronger al-
legiance to their disciplines than to their own peoples. This, he
argued, was frightening because one might then conclude that "in
a crisis they will side with the Whites and will not, under most
circumstances, do anything to help Indians."[325]

Here again, he reminds academics and others trained within
the larger society's institutions of their origins and accompanying obligations to their nations. He had little respect for academic
work that was incomprehensible or of no discernable practical
use, dismissing it as nothing more than surrender to mainstream
individualism. He was particularly scornful of those who hopped
on intellectual bandwagons, parroting phrases and concepts to
impress and fit in with institutional norms. While pontificating
about their Native credentials, they built self-referential alliances
that kept them professionally secure, while their communities saw
nothing in return. Native peoples were not invited to join the pe-
culiar minuet danced by white and Native academics whereby each
sought to gain status by association with the other.

In an interview in 2000, Deloria continued to urge Natives
to tackle their nations' pressing problems—repatriation, challenges to bilingual education, confronting those non-Indians
who depict Native peoples as anti-environmentalists, and lack
of respect for Native elders as oral witnesses in litigation. But he
also emphasized that Native writers, teachers, and politicians
needed to do a better job of educating the public about Indigenous rights and epistemologies. "We still have to work hard," he
said, "to entrench ourselves in the public consciousness as good
guys or at least as people who, while we might have rights other
people don't have, nevertheless are entitled to those rights as a
matter of history and law."[326]

Given his understanding of the validity, vitality, and value of Indigenous knowledge about cosmology (star knowledge), biology (plant and animal knowledge), family life (kinship patterns), criminal jurisdiction (warrior societies as the most effective agents of maintaining peace and order), and music (the role that it plays in health and plant growth), he was concerned that Native peoples were not doing a better job of explaining and describing the inherent benefits of all this knowledge.

Not long after he retired in May 2000, Deloria was at a book signing in Rapid City, South Dakota, to discuss two of his most recent books, *Singing for a Spirit* and *Tribes, Treaties, and Constitutional Tribulations*. After describing both books, he urged aspiring Native writers to emulate his approach; that is, to "put knowledge into the hands of ordinary people." He said, "We need to have a whole group of people writing non-fiction." He went on to observe, "Fifteen years ago, Indians began writing poetry— 'I'm an Indian in Gallup and I'm lonely.' We've had years of that and now it is time for Indians to start writing about science and social science."[327]

Deloria was interviewed by Derrick Jensen for the journal *The Sun* in 2000. Titled "Where the Buffalo Go: How Science Ignores the Living World," the two covered a range of topics in a free-swinging conversation. Jensen's opening question set a philosophical tone for the interview: "What," said Jensen, "would you say is the fundamental difference between the Western and Indigenous ways of life?" Deloria responded,

> I think the primary difference is that Indians experience and relate to a living universe, whereas Western people—especially scientists—reduce all things, living or not, to objects. The implications of this are immense. If you see the world around you as a collection of objects for you to manipulate and exploit, you will inevitably destroy the world while attempting to control it. Not only that, but by perceiving the world as lifeless, you rob yourself of the richness, beauty, and wisdom to be found by participating in its larger design.[328]

After a wide-ranging discussion of the central differences between Western epistemologies and Indigenous ways of knowing, the interview ended with Jensen asking Deloria: "What, then, to an Indian, is the ultimate goal of life?" Deloria's brilliant response harkened back to his articulation in *The Metaphysics of Modern Existence*:

> Maturity: the ability to reflect on the ordinary aspects of life and discover their real meaning. Now, I know this sounds as abstract as anything ever said by a Western scientist or philosopher, but within the context of Indian experience, it isn't abstract at all. Maturity is a matter of reflection on a lifetime of experience, as a person first gathers information, then knowledge, then wisdom. Information accumulates until it achieves a sort of critical mass, and patterns and explanations begin to appear. This is where Western science derives its "laws," but scientists abort the process there, assuming that the products of their own minds are inherent to the structure of the universe. Indians, on the other hand, allow the process to continue, because premature analysis leads to incomplete understanding. When we reach a very old age, or otherwise attain the capacity to reflect on our experiences—most often through visions—we begin to understand how experience, individuality, and the cycles of nature all relate to each other. That state seems to produce wisdom. Because Western society concentrates so heavily on information, its product is youth, not maturity. The existence of thousands of plastic surgeons in America attests to the fact that we haven't crossed the emotional barriers that keep us from experiencing maturity.[329]

In 2001, Deloria contributed a short essay to Serle Chapman's edited volume, *We, The People*, in which he strongly encouraged Native nations to establish viable research institutions. He saw this as an avenue to develop and analyze the kinds of data that would inform reports and policy statements on the myriad issues that affect Indian Country. These materials could be used to educate their own citizenry, the public, and the federal and state governments.

He emphasized that at that time there was too much "talk" about tribal sovereignty and not enough "exercise" of this inherent communal force. "There are hundreds of conferences on sovereignty where people just get up and talk and talk and talk and talk, but very few will do the hard work to go out and exercise the sovereignty that already exists. They spend all of their time trying to define sovereignty more clearly and that's absurd if sovereignty means that any political entity can negotiate on an equal basis with any other. Period.... So sit down and work out a deal!"[330]

He ended the piece with two suggestions for his own people, the Lakota. First, he expressed emphatic support for the revival of the Tiospaye band structure of government, which is based on the kinship patterns of the traditional Lakota communities. Then, he proposed the creation of a new organizational body, the "Sioux Nation," that would be an alliance of all the various Lakota, Dakota, and Nakota bands. This comprehensive entity would then endeavor to renegotiate its treaty relationship with the United States to forge a more realistic and stable political and legal status for the Sioux people and an improved intergovernmental relationship with the federal government.

Interestingly, the broader coalition Deloria envisioned was discussed seriously during the oil and water crisis on and near the Standing Rock Sioux Reservation in the fall of 2016 as the various Sioux bands joined forces, and several Southwestern Native Nations have formed an alliance to protect sacred lands from uranium mining and fossil fuel exploitation.

On the Concept of the Seven Generations

Richard Grounds, George Tinker, and David Wilkins edited a collection of essays in 2003 titled *Native Voices: American Indian Identity and Resistance*[331] in honor of Deloria's prolific list of accomplishments and the profound influence he had on each of the volume's editors and authors. Deloria was invited to write the concluding chapter.

His essay, "The Passage of Generations," was written in a brutally somber tone in which he bemoaned his lack of ability to understand the views and motivations of the current crop of Native writers trying to show their respect for him. He remarked in his introduction, "I thank them for the compliments, most of which are not deserved, and for helping me hide the quirks in my personality and the many failures I have experienced along the way."[332] Vine was a well-mannered person but aware that like all human beings he, too, had an ego. At once surprisingly modest and understandably proud about his talents and accomplishments, he continuously worked to balance the two.

Despite this apparent generation gap, Deloria proceeded to make several suggestions that could produce useful strategies and information. His opening salvo focused, not surprisingly, on treaties. He lauded small Northwest Native nations—Lummi, Puyallup, and Skokomish—for leveraging their treaties in ways that benefited all Native people. He contrasted their decisions with other nations: "I often wonder what Indian affairs would be like if the large land-based tribes had been aggressive about treaty provisions in the past four decades. Would we have a much different perspective on self-government and the inherent power of Indian treaties?"[333]

He then pronounced that Natives needed to do a much better job of deconstructing the meaning of consent, a major concept that he had long championed. He said that "until we develop the scholarly literature that can transform consent into a legal requirement, we would not have made much progress in Indian law."[334] Thirteen years later, in a 2016 lecture at Evergreen State College, Deloria's friend Hank Adams raised this same critical point, saying within the context of a discussion of environmental issues that today tribal consultation was considered adequate for the federal government to proceed with a given project, when the real requirement should be tribal consent.

Finally, and in keeping with his later scholarship on the strength, beauty, and utility of traditional Indigenous knowledge, he noted that "Indian traditions may become an important part of the new scientific paradigm that will seek to give a better exploration of the history of our planet."[335] Acknowledging that much of that knowledge was no longer available, he still believed that the next generation of Natives had a duty to "articulate tribal traditions…" and "make Indian knowledge important to others."[336]

The World We Used to Live in: Remembering the Powers of the Medicine Men (2006) was virtually completed just before Deloria died in November 2005. It is a stunning collection of accounts from a variety of Native holy people, anthropologists, missionaries, Native scholars, and others, designed to inspire its Native audience to seek knowledge and power from their ancestral traditions. Deloria's eldest son, Philip, observed in his preface that it "offers a befitting capstone to his career, for it encapsulates those multiplicities [types of knowledge, different groups of people, and distinctive visions of the future], while also returning to the root, the core, the bedrock—his own faith in the powers that exist in the world and in the ability of Indian people to draw upon them as resources for Indian futures."[337]

Although Deloria said his book was but "a sketch of a vast field of inquiry," it is a broad and thorough review by a gifted philosopher that "demonstrates to the present and coming generations the sense of humility, the reliance of the spirits, and the immense powers that characterized our people in the old days."[338] Equally important, he hoped that it would "inspire people to treat their ceremonies with more respect and to seek out the great powers that are always available to people who look first to the spirits and then to their own resources."[339]

Another of Deloria's books, *C. G. Jung and the Sioux Traditions* (2009), was published after his death.[340] He had worked on this project since the 1980s, never satisfied that it was complete. It is a fascinating comparative study of Jungian psychiatry and Lakota intellectual and spiritual traditions.

He was entranced by this particular Western philosopher because "Jung was seeking to supplant the history, religion, philosophy and educational traditions of the West with a new synthesis, with psychology as its focus and psychological analysis as its methodological tool. This ambitious goal—creating a new synthe-

sis of knowledge—is precisely what makes Jungian psychology …
the best candidate for comparison and dialogue with American
Indian beliefs and practices."[341]

One area of agreement between the two cosmologies was their
understanding of the importance of family and how personal
development is deeply interconnected with the past, present, and
future generations. Deloria, of course, was convinced that Lakota
traditions of respecting multiple generations simultaneously was a
necessary and important corrective that he believed could "deep-
en Carl Jung's insights" and by extension, that of all humanity.[342]

The Lakota tenet he chose to analyze was the familiar, but
commonly misinterpreted, concept of Seven Generations,
whereby each generation of Lakota was obligated to consider the
impacts their decisions might have on seven generations of their
family line.

This phrase, *seven generations*, has become ubiquitous in
Indian Country and across the larger society, with the erroneous
understanding that it means acting in a way that sets the stage
for only the *future* seven generations, most of them unknow-
able descendants, who will live decades ahead of the current
time. Deloria pointed out this was a gross simplification of the
responsibilities to maintain past and present as well as future
family bonds.

To take a linear view, looking only to the future, is to neglect
ancestors and immediate kinfolk. This ignores the multilayered
complexity of the Lakota world and the critical role deceased
ancestors play in daily life. The mangled concept thus becomes
one-dimensional and feeds the stereotype of Indians as noble,
self-sacrificing mystics with superhuman visionary powers.

For the Lakota, the tenet had its roots in the multigenerational
and complex living system that embraced each Lakota citizen.
Deloria used the famous Lakota chief Red Cloud as an example.
When negotiating for the Black Hills in the 1860s with the federal
government, Deloria explained, "if a person lived the proper life,
he or she could expect to know, while a child, his or her great-
grandparents and, while an elder, to know his or her great-grandchildren. Any individual, then, could imagine three generations
back and three generations forward, for a total of seven."[343] Such a

continuum of relatives meant that "a person must therefore act so that their great-grandparents would not be ashamed of what they were doing in the present and so that their great-grandchildren could point with pride at what their ancestors had done."[344]

Red Cloud let the US treaty negotiators know that his dedication to the seven generations principle and his insistence that the federal government be held to the same multigenerational standard was vital, because it would ensure the vitality of the Lakota way of life by reminding everyone that "the generations were tied together as if they were all present in the flesh."[345]

Jung, while not featuring the comprehensive multigenerational paradigm of Red Cloud, certainly understood the value of family and ancestry. He noted that

> if our impressions are too distinct we are held to the hour and minute of the present and have no way of knowing how our ancestral psyches listen to and understand the present.... Thus, we remain ignorant of whether our ancestral components find an elementary gratification in our lives or whether they are repelled. Inner peace and contentment depend in large measure upon whether or not the historical family which is inherent in the individual can be harmonized with the ephemeral conditions of the present.[346]

Jung understood that personal development involved a reconciliation of the ancestral past with the present, and he knew that family, kinship, and institutions—the crucial social systems—played a central role in one's efforts to harmonize the past with one's unique ancestry.

While discerning fascinating similarities in Jungian and Lakota cosmologies, Deloria was also fully aware that the two remained dramatically different and that there was "a huge gulf between their foundation and premises."[347] A central difference was the Lakota refusal to separate their thoughts into distinctive categories and disciplines. "Everything," for the Lakota, "was practical, economic, political and religious all at once."[348] Furthermore, the Lakota viewed virtually everything as a matter of personal relationship, while Jung, relying upon the scientific methodology, emphasized the need for objectivity.

Nevertheless, and in clear recognition of the existing differences, Deloria believed that useful parallels could be made between Jungian and Lakota bodies of knowledge, if one could escape the barriers of culture and knowledge. Such a synthesis, though challenging, would prove useful in helping to forge a more comprehensive understanding of the self, community, and universe that would benefit the Lakota and all others.

Chapter 4

LIGHTING THE WAY AHEAD

Conclusion

In 2003, three years after he had retired from the University of Colorado, several former CU colleagues—David H. Getches, Charles Wilkinson, and Patricia Limerick—and three other distinguished Native thinkers—John Echohawk (founder and director of the Native American Rights Fund), Rennard Strickland (former dean of the University of Oregon Law School and a well-known scholar of federal Indian law), and Rebecca Tsosie (a respected Native law professor at the University of Arizona) nominated Deloria for the degree of Doctor of Humane Letters at the University of Colorado.

Getches, who drafted the nominating letter, said that his nomination of Deloria was "especially satisfying because I have known him for more than thirty years and (like virtually everyone who deals in Indian matters) have followed his multi-faceted and inspiring career. As a result, I feel especially confident in my judgment that he is richly deserving of this high honor."[349] After summarizing Deloria's storied activist and scholastic achievements and then commenting on the other letter writers he had tapped for endorsements, Getches concluded his letter by stating that "in my judgment, these supporting letters from such distinguished writers make it ever more clear that Professor Deloria must be counted as one of America's most valuable public intellectuals" and that Deloria was "the nation's preeminent American Indian scholar."[350]

Even as Getches was formulating his letter on behalf of Deloria, the university was embroiled in a major sports scandal with several women stating they had been raped or sexually harassed by CU football players and recruits between 1997 and 2001. In February 2003, university president Elizabeth Hoffman announced that an independent commission appointed by the Board of Regents would investigate the prosecutor's allegations that CU's athletic department used sex and alcohol as recruiting tools. At the end of the month, Governor Bill Owens appointed Attorney General Ken Salazar as special prosecutor to investigate the scandal.

In May, Salazar decided against filing criminal charges in nine alleged sexual assaults involving CU football players. Two weeks later, the Regents released a report saying that although there was evidence that drugs and alcohol were used to entice athletic recruits, there was no suggestion that university officials condoned the misconduct. The university then reinstated the embattled football coach Gary Barnett, and said that no one would be fired because of the scandal. President Hoffman then announced changes that were designed to increase accountability in the athletics department.[351]

On March 6, 2004, President Hoffman sent a letter to Deloria informing him that the Board of Regents had voted to confer an Honorary Doctor of Humane Letters on him at the university's upcoming commencement exercise in December. Deloria responded to Hoffman on May 21 and declined the invitation to accept the degree. He said, "in view of the behavior of university officials and the members of the Board of Regents, I feel I cannot accept this degree." He continued, "I am greatly disturbed by the actions of university officials and the Board of Regents in such a transparent cover-up of the alleged scandals in the athletic department. As a scholar I am dismayed at the use of language to obscure the facts and the intent to continue practices that reflect badly on the university."[352]

Drawing upon his knowledge of legal procedures learned at CU as a law student, Deloria declared that the "reports of the District Attorney's and Attorney General that state insufficient evidence to convict do not mean a clean bill of health or innocence. They simply mean that one or two more bits of evidence and charges might possibly be filed against those being investigated. My education at the School of Law … taught me the difference and perhaps yourself and the Regents should attend some classes on ethics there to clarify your thinking."[353]

Deloria's spurning of his alma mater's honorific title reflects the high ethical standards that he embodied on both the personal and professional levels. He held institutions, especially institutions of higher education and their leaders, to similarly high standards because, in his opinion, they were "supposed to reflect the highest values and beliefs that our society can give so that society can find its way to creating and enjoying a civil society."

Scouting the Unmarked Trail:
An Unfinished Agenda

Although long retired, Deloria was anything but retiring, as a short document he wrote and had placed in his personal files in 2003 attests. Called simply "Vine's Projects," it laid out the work agenda he had set for himself for the immediate future.[354] These records are useful to us as a guide for future action.

The first set of assignments he intended to keep working on were the "Traditional Knowledge Gatherings" he had begun in 1992. He had organized seven gatherings—plant knowledge, animals, techniques of preserving oral traditions, origins and migrations, giants and little people, and two on the subject of Indigenous star knowledge.

The conferences, largely attended by Natives, had been very successful, and he planned to convene several more over the next several years. In keeping with the oral traditions approach that he respected, he encouraged those in attendance to not use electronic recording devices or even take notes on what they heard. In theory, this was a thoughtful gesture, but one wonders what was lost by not having recorded or videotaped the events. Many of the Native presenters have since passed away, and the knowledge they shared at the gatherings may have passed with them.

The next gathering he planned was to feature Indigenous elders and historians who were to talk about their knowledge of volcanoes. As he put it, "It is known from traditional stories that Indians witnessed the Mt. Shasta/Crater Lake eruption around 4,000 B.C. What about other areas and other volcanoes?" His goal was to include ten speakers, and one of the essential questions to be addressed was how Indigenous knowledge supports or challenges existing scientific interpretations of volcanic eruptions.

He next envisioned two other gatherings: one focused on nutrition, the other on medicine. In his own words, "The Native community is at a critical juncture, looking for a balance between protecting traditional medicines from exploitation, and at the same time providing help and cures. Also, the diets of many Native people changed so drastically (government commodities, stealing of previous life ways), the result is a 'health crisis' in Indian Country." Deloria planned to invite Native women from several communities who were involved in health-related work and who had knowledge of traditional foods and medicine to be key presenters.[355]

Other ideas were being considered as well, including gatherings on the sacredness of water and how it relates to fish and plant habitats, and a gathering on buffalo to address that iconic animal's spiritual significance and the attempts of numerous Native nations to engage in sustainable herding and ranching for economic purposes. Deloria ended that section stating that "there are many timely and important topics, and instead of seven over the past fifteen years, we should be planning at least two every year."[356]

"Timely and important," indeed, as witnessed by two recent events in Indian Country. First, in 2014, eleven Native nations, including the Blackfeet, Assiniboine and Gros Ventre, and Salish and Kootenai; and First Nations, including the Blood Tribe, Siksika Nation, and Tsuu T'ina Nation entered into an international treaty called The Buffalo: A Treaty of Cooperation, Renewal and Repatriation, designed to rekindle and strengthen the relationship between their nations and their spiritual, economic, and cultural bonds with this majestic mammal. Second, the principled stand taken by the Standing Rock Sioux, self-identified as "Water Protectors," in the face of an energy company's desire to complete construction of an oil pipeline under the Missouri River, attests to the crucial importance of water to not only Native lives but to the lives of all beings.

Next, Deloria described a documentary on Lakota treaty history he was working on with Raymond DeMallie of Indiana University. Deloria knew there was a need to digitize and make available all the recorded treaty and agreement transcripts, biographies of prominent Lakota leaders, maps of the occupancy area, Court of Claims and Indian Claims Commission materials, and other relevant data. He knew that such a project would have enormous educational value, especially to students in tribal colleges and in high schools with Native students across the country.

Yet another venture he envisioned was an Oratory project to culminate in a book featuring speeches by Indigenous speakers emphasizing the eloquence and meaning of traditional Native oratory. As Deloria put it, "Speeches at treaty meetings were particularly eloquent and their speeches give us great insight into the beliefs and expectations of the leaders when confronted with the necessity of surrendering land and then freedom."[357] This was to be a major project that would begin with Lakota documents but then expand to Record Group 75—the major group of documents in the National Archives containing treaty materials. The final set of documents to be compiled would be those made by Natives when they testified at the ten Indian Congresses held throughout the United States when John Collier was drumming up support for the Indian Reorganization Act.

The study would stress the worldview of individual Native speakers, highlighting and analyzing their philosophies and intents as they prepared to sign a particular treaty or agreement, or express support or disfavor for the IRA. Deloria also planned to oversee a Native student oratory contest at an Indian-controlled high school or tribal college.

Several non-Native historians—Dan Flores, Elliot West, and Shepherd Kretch—had written recent accounts that lay the decimation of buffalo herds on Native hunters rather than on white

hunters. Deloria was convinced these individuals had manipu-
lated the evidence to arrive at their conclusions, and he was aware
that their work had been cited by anti-Indian groups who were
opposed to the important work being done by the InterTribal
Bison Cooperative (ITBC), a coalition of more than forty Native nations who are keen on raising buffalo in a sustainable and
respectable fashion.

The project's goal was to hire an individual who would work
with the ITBC to collect their data and then write a reasoned and
dispassionate account that accurately discussed the history of the
buffalo, the reasons for their precipitous decline, and what needed
to be done to continue their recovery. This work would then be
used to refute the inaccurate studies prepared by non-Indian
writers and to educate the public about the unique relationship
between Native peoples and buffalo.[358]

Deloria also knew that children needed to receive more attention, and he had plans for a series of children's books that would
not only be about Native children but would, in fact, be created
by the children themselves. "The purpose," he said, "is to provide
Indian children the opportunity to share their talents, worldviews,
and to make learning fun. Gaining confidence in their place
in society will provide the bridge to higher education outside
the community."[359] These books were to involve language skills,
artistic talents, and the relaying of stories. The students were to
be encouraged to express traditional knowledge in the text and
via images. Aware that K–12 teachers were already overburdened
with many duties, Deloria knew that this project would need a
great deal of outside financial support. Moreover, he conceived
this as a project that would move from reservation to reservation,
depending on interest levels.

Within the corpus of his work, Vine Deloria Jr. forged a comprehensive and interrelated set of ideas meant to provide ongoing
vision, strength, and protection for Indigenous nationhood. He
definitively articulated the right and reality of tribal sovereignty
and its life-giving force of self-determination. He left us astute
analyses of the fundamental importance of space and place to
Native nations, and of the principle of interdependency. And he
charged each of us to work toward maturity.

Based on these tenets, he crafted accompanying recommendations for the federal (and state) government and Indigenous nations that, if enacted, would go far toward stabilizing and clarifying the cultural identities, political and legal standing, and territorial basis of Native nations.

In the broadest sense, not only would these suggestions strengthen Indigenous nationhood, they would also fortify the notion of the United States as a pluralistic democracy, home to not one, but rather many democracies, including those of Indigenous nations.

This book began with a descriptive analysis of Deloria's ideas for actions to be taken by the federal government, including, but not limited to, formal acknowledgment of tribal sovereignty, revival of the treaty process, renouncement of congressional plenary power (read: absolute), continuation and expedition of the consolidation and restoration of Native lands, affirmation of the rights of bona fide eastern (and other) Native nations to full recognition by the federal government, establishment of a permanent Court of Indian Affairs, support for the international and domestic status of tribal nations, transformation of the trust doctrine from active to passive, recognition of the legitimacy of Native oral testimony in federal courts and legislative halls, and a host of others aimed at improving the perpetually beleaguered BIA.

We then turned to his internal critiques and a set of pronouncements for Native nations, which included the ongoing search for meaning and relevancy for tribal nations in the twentieth and twenty-first centuries and the urgent need to overcome the many entrenched bifurcations that weaken and destabilize Indian Country—urban Indian youth/reservation-based elders, urban/reservation communities, eastern/western Native peoples, recognized/nonrecognized, and traditional/ethnic.

Deloria offered ideas on the teaching of traditional knowledge, values, and traditions to Indigenous youth, as well as on improving and making more accountable Indigenous educational, political, and cultural figures. His templates to strengthen tribal governments, consolidate tribal property, develop an Indigenous common law, use social media more appropriately, and improve Native political and economic relations with other polities remain valid and practical.

As noted, some of Deloria's suggestions have found their way into law, policy, and popular discourse. But many remain to be taken up by Indigenous communities, Native leaders, or state and national lawmakers.

As we stride deeper into the twenty-first century, with changes in philosophy, the environment, and geopolitics driven ever more rapidly by technology, we must unite and organize Native America across every sphere: economics, science, culture, family life, politics, and law—Deloria's ideas offer us a shared template for this undertaking.

The fact that we still have so far to go in the face of so many obstacles, both old and new, can be disheartening, but we have been given the knowledge to defend and improve our nations. Deloria's canon is an important part of that legacy. Let us wield these tools as they have been proposed and retain the power to unite our peoples for our own collective survival as nations and to improve the human condition and protect the natural world.

Afterword

In the introduction to his 2002 book *Evolution, Creationism, and Other Modern Myths*, Vine Deloria Jr. noted, "I offer no comfort to religious fundamentalists or evolutionists. The views of both are passé and represent only a quarrel within the Western belief system, not an accurate reflection of Earth history." It was a vintage Vine moment, poking a finger in the eye of the intellectual establishment and, more importantly, challenging readers to think beyond their established beliefs. At this point, I had been working with Vine for more than a decade, and yet his ability to elegantly force us to rethink dogma with a twinkle of humor in his eye still impressed me.

Upon his passing, many newspaper obituaries commented on Vine's skill at challenging common myths about American Indians. His goal, according to the *New York Times* (paraphrasing Vine) was to "instill [in Indian audiences] a belief in a culture that had been shattered by history, and by deliberate government policy." As David Wilkins skillfully shows us in *Red Prophet*, Vine was highly successful in this endeavor. Vine's words and leadership provided the intellectual core of Indian Country for the latter half of the twentieth and early twenty-first centuries. And Vine certainly recognized the impact. As he explained to me once, "Every time a negative review of one of my books appears in the mainstream press, book sales explode among Indians." The importance of his contributions to Indian Country, raising consciousness for millions of Indigenous peoples in America and around the globe, discussing everything from policies to treaties to the relationship of Indians and the natural world, cannot be overstated. He was, in the words of law professor (and good friend of Vine) Charles Wilkinson, "the most important person in Indian affairs [during the past century] period."

In addition to his essential intellectual leadership in Indian Country, Vine also recognized that after the initial reaction to his books settled, non-Indians would actually pick them up and discover that he had something important to say. While many memorialized Vine for his impact on the marginalized Indigenous peoples of North America and their history and culture, he also wrote broadly on science, religion, education, and philosophy. The challenge of looking at any leader of a minority culture in the United States is the tendency for broader society to view this person solely through the lens of their own culture. We tend to look at such people as great "fill in the blanks with cultural identity" thinkers (in Vine's case, a great "Native American" thinker), when in fact, many times their contributions are much larger than this. It is my opinion, shared by many, that Vine Deloria Jr. is truly a great "American" thinker, deserving of inclusion with other scholars and intellectuals whom we continue to read decades and centuries after their passing.

Vine, like these others great American thinkers, deserves to be read by all Americans, regardless of background. In his works on the marginalization of Indians, we can recognize our failure at various points in our history to live up to the ideals upon which the country was founded. In his works on science, we can recognize that the understanding many of us have about our physical world disregards the wisdom of Indigenous peoples. In his works on education, we can recognize the failure of our systems to support minorities and the resulting impacts and challenges for broader society. And in his works on religion and philosophy, we can appreciate that the metaphysical realm is in many ways beyond our understanding, and that we are mere strivers in making sense of the higher planes of our existence. In all cases, Vine forced us to think critically, to challenge our presumed understanding of the world, and to intellectually grow (and grow up) as a result. In the end, I can think of no better way to define a *great* American thinker than this ability to help us understand our common humanity.

About a year before his passing, Vine joined me for lunch with Wilma Mankiller, the groundbreaking former chief of the Cherokee Nation. At one point, I asked both of them what message they wished to convey to younger generations. Vine replied, not missing a beat, that young people needed to get educated and get active in their communities, becoming leaders who could create change from below (Wilma seconded his call to action). When I see young Indians today reading Vine's books, uncovering the essential truths that Vine left for posterity, and sparking the fire to change the world around them, it warms my soul. David Wilkins has done the world a great service with *Red Prophet*. It is my sincere hope that more Americans discover Vine, read his works, agree to be challenged to think critically, and recognize the prophetic words of this great American thinker.

—*Sam Scinta*

Appendix

Curriculum Outline

Problems and Issues
Relating to American Indians

I. Historical Background of American Indians

    (1) Quasi-Independent Political Communities—1492–1815

    (2) Colonial Relations with Indian Tribes—1607–1785

    (3) Post-Revolutionary Period—1785–1815

        a. Treaties and Land Cessions

        b. Trade with Indians

            1. Southern region—Five Civilized Tribes

            2. Ohio Valley—Great Lakes: Chippewa, Ottawa, Potawatomi Miami, Sioux

    (4) Removal Period—1817–1871

        a. Removal of The Five Civilized Tribes—Reestablishment of Governments of the Five Civilized Tribes

        b. Removal from Ohio Valley—Trek to Kansas—Then Oklahoma

    (5) End of Treaty-Making Period—Era of Agreements

        a. 1871—End of Treaties

b.   Agreements—1887 Allotment Act

c.   Statehood of Oklahoma—End of Oklahoma Tribal Government

d.   Final Agreements—1906

(6) A Matter of Administration—1906–1932

a.   1924 Indian Citizenship Act

b.   1924 Pueblo Lands Act

c.   Meriam Study—Pre–New Deal (Indian Reorganization Act)

(7) New Deal Programs—1934–1946

a.   Indian Reorganization Act—1934

b.   Johnson-O'Malley Act—1934

c.   Oklahoma Indian Welfare Act—1936

d.   Indian Claims Commission Act—1946

(8) Post–New Deal Legislation

a.   Navajo-Hopi Rehabilitation Act—1950

b.   Public Law 280—1953

(9) Termination of Federal Supervision—House Concurrent Resolution 108

a.   Menominee Tribe—Wisconsin

b.   Klamath Tribe—Oregon

c.   Mixed-Blood Utes—Utah

d.   Alabama-Coushatta—Texas

e.   Others: Paiutes—Utah; Numerous Rancherias—California Rancherias; Catawba—South Carolina

(10) New Frontier—Great Society Programs

a.   Area Redevelopment Programs—Economic Development Administration

b.   Office of Economic Development

c.   Education Funds—Health, Education, Welfare

d.   National Council on Indian Opportunity

(11) Current Programs and Proposals

    a.   Blue Lake—Taos Pueblo

    b.   Trust Counsel Authority

    c.   Reorganization of Bureau of Indian Affairs

    d.   Water Rights Office

    e.   Settlement of Alaska Native Land Claims

II.   Economic Variety in Indian Tribes

(1) Traditional Economic Systems—Hunting, Fishing, Farming, and Trading

(2) Adapted Economic Patterns—Farming, Lumber, Mining, Wage Work, Commercial Fishing, Small Business, Ranching, Tourism, Nontribal Employment, Nontraditional Employment, Civil Service, Missionary Work, Teaching, and Administration

(3) Contemporary Examples of Tribal Economic Enterprises

    a.   Red Lake Chippewa, Yakima, Quinault, Colville, Navajo—Timber and Related Wood Products

    b.   Red Lake Chippewa, Lummi, Nisqually, Quinault—Fishing Industries

    c.   Yankton Sioux, Navajo, Turtle Mountain Chippewa—Specialty Work: Electronics

    d.   Flathead, White Mountain Apache, Mescalero Apache—Tourism and Recreation Development

    e.   Rosebud Sioux, Fort Peck Sioux, Fort Belknap, Northern Arapaho, San Carlos Apache, Papago (Tohono O'odham)—Ranching

    f.   Colorado River, Salt River, Gila River—Irrigation and Farming

    g.   Oklahoma Tribes—Wage Employment, Tribal Factories

    h.   Jicarilla Apache, Yakima—Movies

(4) Employment Problems

    a.   Relocation Programs—Moving Indians to Cities

      b.   Failure of Factories—Oglala Sioux, Crow Creek Sioux, Coeur d'Alene

      c.   Seasonal Work—Potato Picking, Migrant Labor, Navajo, Colville—Apple Picking

      d.   Educational Handicaps in Administration—Mescalero Apache, Lummi—Stability of Tribal Programs

      e.   Politics of Tribal Programs

      f.   Small Businesses on Reservations

(5) Educational Opportunities

      a.   Lack of Coordination with Tribal Programs

      b.   Lack of Counseling as to Careers

      c.   Restrictions as to Federal Funds—$3 Scholarships, $25 Million to Vocational Training

      d.   Lack of Advanced Training or Education

      e.   No Business Education on Reservations

           1.   No classes in insurance, loans, etc.

           2.   Inability to get information on programs

           3.   Discouragement by the BIA of Indian involvement

III.   Tax Status of American Indians

(1) Exemption from Income Derived from Trust Lands

(2) Exemption, in Some States, From State Sales Tax

(3) Exemption, in Some States, from State Income Tax

(4) Confusion by Indians as to Actual Tax Status

      a.   Detriment to Leasing of Lands

      b.   Detriment to Establishment of Small Businesses

      c.   Refusal of Tribes to Plan Programs

      d.   Fear of Losing Tribal and Individual Lands

      e.   Social Security and Old Age Payments and Trust Lands

      f.   Negative Attitude Exemplified in Tax Confusion

(5) Tribal Services as Form of Taxation

    a.   Tribal Scholarships

    b.   Tribal Employment Programs

    c.   Tribal Sponsorship of Government Programs

    d.   Attitude toward Tribal Services Affects All Conceptions of Tribal Government, the Federal Relationship, and Ultimately the Status of Indian Lands.

IV. Educational Problems

(1) Federal Boarding Schools

    a.   Traditional—Carlisle, Hampton Institute

    b.   Present Generation Looks to Haskell Institute, Kansas

    c.   Attitudes of Older Generation toward Carlisle

    d.   Attitudes of Present Generation toward Boarding Schools—Age Group 30–45, Age Group 15–30

    e.   Inadequacy of Federal Boarding School Concept Today

        1. Pre-truant confinement

        2. Orphanages

        3. Abandonment

        4. Location of boarding schools

            i.   Intermountain School and Navajo

            ii. Chemawa School and Alaska

           iii. Pierre School and Montana Indians

           iv. Stewart School and Nevada-Navajo

(2) Developments in Federal Programs

    a.   Indian Educational Advisory Committee

    b.   Rough Rock Schools—Navajo Reservation

    c.   Santa Fe Art Institute—Arts and Crafts

    d.   Haskell Junior College—Lawrence, Kansas

(3) Failures in Federal Education

      a.   Civil Service Security and Average Age of Educators

      b.   Instability of Teaching Staff on Reservations—the Last or First Stop for Teachers

      c.   Lack of Direction in Educational Philosophy— Education or Creation of "White Red Men"

      d.   The Fear of Continual Investigation by Outsiders

      e.   Failure to Demote or Punish Incompetent Administrators

      f.   Outmoded Disciplinary Practices by Federal Officials

      g.   Failure to Involve Students in Programs

      h.   Incompetency of Studies on Indian Education

(4) State Education of Indians

      a.   Misuse of Johnson-O'Malley Funds

      b.   Refusal to Involve Indian Parents

      c.   The Indian as Athlete

      d.   Counseling at the Local School Level

      e.   Discrimination against Poor Indians, Indians in General

      f.   Attempted Integration of Indians into School System on Artificial Basis

      g.   Lack of Familiarity with Tribal Programs, No Contact with Tribal Council or Tribal Education Committee

      h.   Competing Federal Programs

V.   A Different Social Climate

  (1) Indian Communities

      a.   Tribal Celebrations

      b.   Kinship and Family Systems

      c.   Visiting Patterns, Trips, and Powwows

      d.   Intermarriage

      e.   Customs and Ceremonies

(2) Religious Conflict

    a.   Denominationalism—Competition between Churches

    b.   Mormonism and Loss of Children to Churches

    c.   Paternalism in Church Structures for Natives

    d.   Indian Religious Practices

        1. Giveaways

        2. Peyote

        3. Dances

        4. Handgames

        5. Burials

    e.   Clashes Between Christian and Non-Christian Religions

(3) Divisions in Indian Society

    a.   Full Bloods and Mixed Bloods

    b.   Educated and Uneducated

    c.   Young and Old

    d.   Traditional and Progressive

    e.   Developers and Anti-Development People

    f.   Tribal Politicians and Critics

    g.   Ancient Enmities—Family Feuds—Different Bands on One Reservation—Jealousies

(4) Common Beliefs of Indian Communities

    a.   Feeling of Betrayal by the Federal Government

    b.   Suspicion of New Ideas and Social Movements

    c.   Suspicion of Unions, Organizing Efforts

    d.   Feeling of Betrayal by Senators and Congresspeople

    e.   Feeling That the Tribal Council Is Corrupt

    f.   Feeling Unable to Plan Independent of the BIA

    g.   Resentment at Destruction of Lands and Sacred Places

    h.   Longing for Old Way of Life—Regardless of What Kind of Life That Might Have Been

    i.   Fear of reprisals by BIA, Public Health Service, or Other Agency Personnel

VI. Health Problems

  (1) Facilities

    a.   Isolated Small Communities Preclude Adequate Facilities

    b.   Inadequate Appropriations Preclude Adequate Facilities

    c.   Tendency of Indian Health Service to Use Contracts with City and County Hospitals Is Resented by Indians

  (2) Reservation Problems

    a.   Lack of Telephones, Roads, Communication Infrastructure

    b.   Lack of Adequate Drinking Water, Wells, Sanitation Programs

    c.   Few Preventative Medicine Programs

    d.   Long Distances Preclude Visits to Medical Facilities Except When Situation Is Very Serious

  (3) Health Personnel

    a.   Resentment at Constant Shifting of Doctors, Dentists, Nurses

    b.   Resentment at Lack of Indian Promotion in Nursing Ranks

    c.   Doctors Are Two-Year Alternate Service People—Escaping Draft to Practice on Indians Before They Begin Their Own Practice

  (4) Diet

    a.   Inadequate Nourishment from Commodities

    b.   Low Income Precludes Balanced Diet

    c.   Isolation Increases Costs of Foodstuffs

      d.   Foods of Anglo-Saxon Unusual for Indians Used to Other Diet

  (5) Alcoholism

      a.   Severe Problems in Middle-Age Group

      b.   Broken Homes and Unemployment Due to Alcohol

      c.   Alcohol-Related Accidental Deaths

      d.   Alcohol-Related Suicides

      e.   Alcohol as a Socially Related Activity

VII. The Indian Political Scene

  (1) Iroquois Nationalism—Mad Bear Anderson, The White Roots of Peace, Canadian Influence on Traditionalists

  (2) Traditionalists—Thomas Banyacya, Janet McCloud

  (3) The Five Civilized Tribes—Conservatism in Oklahoma

  (4) Northwest Affiliated Tribes—Conservatism in the Northwest

  (5) National Congress of American Indians—the Oldest Organization, basically Conservative

  (6) National Indian Youth Council—Post–College Age Young People, Programs Against Government Boarding Schools, Employment in Government Agencies

  (7) American Indian Movement—Urban-Based Activists

  (8) Survival of American Indians—Northwest Fishing Rights Struggle, Hank Adams

  (9) United Scholarship Service—Tillie Walker: the Remnants of the Poor People's Campaign

  (10) American Indian Law Students—Core Group of Indians Educated for Professional Work

  (11) Americans for Indian Opportunity—Oklahomans for Indian Opportunity: LaDonna Harris, Labor Unions, Movie Stars

  (12) California Inter-Tribal Council—Mixture of Urban and Small Reservation Indians

VIII. Alaska

   (1)   The Alaska Native Claims Settlement Act

       a.   Conflict between Indians and Inuit

       b.   Villages vs. Corporations

       c.   Two Conceptions of Land

       d.   Investment of Cash Received in Settlement

   (2)   Alaskan Organizations

       a.   Alaska Native Brotherhood—Oldest Organization

       b.   Tlingit-Haida General Council

       c.   Alaska Federation of Natives—Group Forcing Settlement

   (3)   Immediate Problems

       a.   Change from Hunting to Urban Culture

       b.   Education Away from Native Culture

       c.   Lack of Employment Opportunities

       d.   Conflict with State Over Hunting and Fishing Rights

       e.   Isolation of Villages from Alaskan Society and Urban Centers

   (4)   Alaskan Leaders

       a.   William Hensley—State Legislator

       b.   Charles Edwardson—Inuit

       c.   Donald Wright—Urban Native

       d.   John Borbridge—Indian

IX. Summary

   (1)   Current Problems with Federal Government

       a.   Water Rights

       b.   Tribal Self-Government

       c.   Reservation Control of Schooling

       d.   Long-Term Leasing for Development

       e.   Establishment of Trust Authority

(2) Indian Activism

    a.   Public Relations of Urban Indians

    b.   Religious Orientation of Activists

    c.   Land Restoration as Goal

    d.   Establishment of Indian Schools and Housing Programs in Urban Areas

    e.   Fight against Rigidity of Federal Boarding School System

(3) Current Coalitions

    a.   Combination of NCAI, NIYC, AIM—Wide Area of Programs

    b.   Willingness to Enter Coalitions Outside Indian Affairs

    c.   Political Orientation—Left of Center but Basically Conservative—Percy Republicans

    d.   Stability of Current Coalition—Building for Greater Political Strength—Based on Indian Religion

NOTES

1. Charles A. Eastman, "The Soul of the Indian: An Interpretation" (Lincoln: University of Nebraska Press, 1911. Republished in 1980), 157.

2. Vine Deloria Jr. and David E. Wilkins, *Tribes, Treaties, and Constitutional Tribulations* (Austin: University of Texas Press, 1999), and *The Legal Universe: Observations on the Foundations of American Law* (Golden, CO: Fulcrum Publishing, 2011).

3. Personal correspondence, August 22, 1994.

4. Ibid.

5. Ibid.

6. Personal correspondence, August 2, 2004.

7. Roger Dunsmore, "Vine Deloria, Jr. (March 26, 1933–)," in Andrew Wiget, ed., *Handbook of Native American Literature* (New York: Garland Publishing, Inc., 1996), 411–415; Bruce E. Johansen, ed., "Vine Deloria, Jr. (b. 1933)," in Bruce E. Johansen, *Shapers of the Great Debate on Native Americans Land, Spirit, and Power: A Bibliographical Dictionary* (Westport, CT: Greenwood Press, 2000), 210–216; David Deleon, "Vine Deloria, Jr. (1933–)," in David Deleon, ed., *Leaders from the 1960s: A Biographical Sourcebook of American Activism* (Westport, CT: Greenwood Press, 1994), 72–78; Karen P. Zimmerman, "Vine Deloria, Jr., 1933–," in Sharon Malinowski, ed., *Notable Native Americans* (New York: Gale Research Inc., 1994), 118–121; David H. Dejong, "Choosing the Red Road: Family Legacy, Leadership, and Vine Deloria, Jr.," in *Red Ink*, vol. 14, no. 1 (Spring 2008): 86–94; Sidner Larson, *Captured in the Middle: Tradition and Experience in Contemporary Native American Writing* (Seattle: University of Washington Press, 2015), 58–69; Steve Pavlik, "WSSA Loses Longtime Friend & Supporter," *Western Social Science Association News*, vol. 38, no. 2 (Spring 2006): 1, 6; Troy A. Richardson, "Vine Deloria, Jr. as a Philosopher of Education: An Essay in Remembrance," *Anthropology and Education Quarterly*, vol. 38, no. 3 (2007): 221–230; Bryan McKinley Brayboy, K. Tsianina Lomawaima, and Malia Villegas, "The Lives and Work of Beatrice Medicine and Vine Deloria, Jr.," *Anthropology & Education Quarterly*, vol. 38, no. 3 (2007):

231–238; Frederick E. Hoxie, "Indian American or American Indian? Vine Deloria, Jr., Sioux," in Frederick E. Hoxie, *This Indian Country: American Indian Activists and the Place They Made* (New York: Penguin Press, 2012), 337–392; Michael Anthony Lawrence, "Vine Deloria, Jr. (1933–2005): Betrayals and Bridges," in *Radicals in Their Own Time, Four Hundred Years of Struggle for Liberty and Equal Justice in America* (New York: Cambridge University Press, 2011), 245–308; James Treat, "Introduction: An American Critique of Religion," in Vine Deloria Jr., *For This Land: Writings on Religion in America* (New York: Routledge Press, 1999), 1–18; and Robert A. Warrior, *Tribal Secrets: Recovering American Indian Intellectual Traditions* (Minneapolis: University of Minnesota Press, 1995).

8. Vine Deloria Jr., *Singing for a Spirit: A Portrait of the Dakota Sioux* (Santa Fe, NM: Clear Light Publishers, 2000), 6–87.

9. Raymond J. DeMallie, "Vine Deloria, Jr. (1933–2005)," *American Anthropologist*, vol. 108, no. 4 (2006): 932.

10. See the outstanding "Part I: Vision and Prophecy," in Vine Deloria Jr.'s *Singing for a Spirit: A Portrait of the Dakota Sioux* (Santa Fe, NM: Clear Light Publishers, 2000), which is an intimate genealogical account of the Deloria family from the 1700s to the twentieth century.

11. Ibid.

12. Michael Anthony Lawrence, *Radicals in Their Own Time: Four Hundred Years of Struggle for Liberty and Equal Justice in America* (New York: Cambridge University Press, 2011), 261.

13. Statement of Vine Deloria, Jr. "To the Opportunity Fellowships, John Hay Whitney Foundation" (dated 1952). Author has copy of the letter.

14. Ibid.

15. DeMallie, "Vine Deloria, Jr.," 932.

16. Vine Deloria, Jr. to Bob (no last name), February 9, 1973. Author has copy of letter.

17. Letter from Robert L. Rosenthal, chairman, board of directors, United Scholarship Service. September 4, 1967. Author has copy of letter.

18. Rykken Johnson, "Author Discusses Indian Activism," *Rocky Mountain News*, November 1, 1969, p. 55.

19. Vine Deloria, Jr. to George E. Troutt III, August 17, 1969. Author has copy of letter.

20. Ibid.

21. Vine Deloria Jr. to Robert Lane, September 17, 1969. Author has copy of letter.

22. Ibid.

23. Vine Deloria, Jr. to the Rev. G. H. Jack Woodard, September 1, 1969. Author has copy of letter.

24. Ibid.

25. Vine Deloria Jr. to John Hadsell, April 25, 1973. Author has copy of letter.

26. Ibid., 2.

27. DeMallie, "Vine Deloria, Jr.," 933.

28. Edward W. Said, *Representations of the Intellectual* (New York: Vintage Books, 1994), 53.

29. Ibid., 64.

30. Vine Deloria Jr., *Custer Died for Your Sins* (Norman: University of Oklahoma Press, 1969, 1988), 144–145.

31. 88 Stat. 2203.

32. Vine Deloria Jr., "But It Was All Ad Hoc: Comment on Gullickson's Paper," *Native American Studies*, vol. 7, no. 1 (1993): 7.

33. Vine Deloria Jr., *The Metaphysics of Modern Existence* (Golden, CO: Fulcrum Publishing, 2012), 287–288.

34. Ibid., 288.

35. Christopher Stone, *Should Trees Have Standing? Law, Morality, and the Environment*, 3rd ed. (New York: Oxford University Press, 2010).

36. Deloria, *The Metaphysics of Modern Existence*, 288.

37. Ibid., 289.

38. Deloria, "But It Was All Ad Hoc," 7–8.

39. Victor Riesel, "Inside Labor," Hall Syndicate, February 13, 1965.

40. 82 Stat. 73.

41. US Congress. Senate. Hearings Before the Subcommittee on Constitutional Rights of the Committee on the Judiciary on S. 961, S. 962, etc., "Constitutional Rights of the American Indian," 89th Cong., 1st Sess. (January 22, 1965), 196.

42. 107 Stat. 2004.

43. 114 Stat. 2778.

44. Ibid.

45. 124 Stat. 2258.

46. Deloria, *Custer Died for Your Sins*, 27.

47. Ibid., 51.

48. Ibid., 52.

49. Ibid.

50. Bruce Granville Miller, *Invisible Indigenes: The Politics of Nonrecognition* (Lincoln: University of Nebraska Press, 2003). Still, the Department of Interior did amend the criteria in 2014, thus making it a little less onerous for nonrecognized groups to meet the required criteria to become a federally recognized tribal entity by making the process "more transparent, promote consistent implementation, while maintaining the integrity of the process," *US Federal Register*, "Federal Acknowledgment of American Indian Tribes," vol. 79, no. 103 (Thursday, May 29, 2014).

51. V. Deloria, *Custer Died for Your Sins*, 136.

52. 88 Stat. 2203.

53. Ibid., 144.

54. Ibid., 142.

55. Ibid., 143.

56. Ibid., 258.

57. Vine Deloria Jr., *We Talk, You Listen: New Tribes, New Turf* (New York: Macmillan, 1970), 107.

58. Ibid., 117–118.

59. Ibid.

60. Ibid., 121.

61. Ibid., 190.

62. Vine Deloria Jr. to Jack Greenberg, November 3, 1969. Author has copy of letter.

63. Monroe E. Price, *Law and the American Indian: Readings, Notes, and Cases* (Indianapolis: The Bobbs-Merrill Company, 1973).

64. Vine Deloria Jr. to Sanford Smith, February 5, 1970. Author has copy of letter.

65. Vine Deloria Jr. to William L. Paddock, March 19, 1970. Author has copy of letter.

66. Vine Deloria Jr., *Of Utmost Good Faith* (San Francisco: Straight Arrow Books, 1971), 60.

67. Ibid., 1.

68. 114 Stat. 2019.

69. "Big Foot Riders Remember Wounded Knee," *Indian Country Today* (January 3, 2003), 1.

70. Vine Deloria Jr. to Dan Smith, January 1970. Author has copy of letter.

71. Vine Deloria Jr. to Charles Kettering II, March 24, 1971. Author has copy of letter.

72. Ibid.

73. Vine Deloria Jr., "The BIA: My Brother's Keeper," *Art in America* (July–August, 1972): 115.

74. Ibid.

75. Vine Deloria Jr. to Jeanette Smith, April 13, 1972. Author has copy of letter.

76. Ibid.

77. Ibid.

78. Edgar Cahn, *Our Brother's Keeper: The Indian in White America* (New York: World Publishing Co., 1969).

79. Vine Deloria Jr. to Ralph Nader, August 1, 1972. Author has copy of letter.

80. Vine Deloria Jr., *God Is Red: A Native View of Religion* (Golden, CO: Fulcrum Publishing, 1994), 89.

81. Vine Deloria Jr., "'White Society Is Breaking Down Around Us ... Even Its Myths—Like the Melting Pot—Are Dead': An Interview with American Indian Writer Vine Deloria Jr," by Peter Collier. *Mademoiselle*, vol. 72 (April 1971): 202–204, 269.

82. Vine Deloria Jr., "Interview with Vine Deloria," *Akwesasne Notes* (Early Winter 1973), n.p.

83. 102 Stat. 2285.

84. 108 Stat. 4250.

85. Vine Deloria Jr., *Los Angeles Times*, April 1, 1973.

86. Report contained in the documents received by the author from the FBI via Freedom of Information Act request, March 30, 2010.

87. Vine Deloria Jr. to LaDonna Harris, October 10, 1973. Author has copy of letter.

88. Ibid.

89. Ibid.

90. Vine Deloria Jr., *Behind the Trail of Broken Treaties: An Indian Declaration of Independence* (New York: Delacorte Press, 1974), 278, 252.

91. Ibid., 253.

92. Ibid.

93. Ibid., 254.

94. This resolution was introduced by representatives Keith Kempenich and Vicky Steiner.

95. See *US v. Consolidated Wounded Knee Cases*, 389 F. Supp. 235 (1975) and *US v. Dodge*, 538 F.2d 770 (1976).

96. Vine Deloria Jr., interview with Vine Deloria Jr., by Larry Leventhal, August 5, 2009.

97. Randy Furst, "Larry Leventhal, Attorney Who Championed American Indian Rights, Dies at 75," *Star Tribune* (Minneapolis) (January 17, 2017), http://www.startribune.com/larry-leventhal-attorney-whochampioned-American-Indian-rights-dies-at-75/410949245/.

98. Ibid.

99. Leventhal interview, 2009.

100. Vine Deloria Jr., "The Next Three Years," *The Indian Historian*, vol. 7, no. 1 (Winter 1974): 26.

101. Ibid., 53.

102. Vine Deloria Jr. to Kent B. Connally, January 25, 1974. Author has copy of letter.

103. Vine Deloria Jr., *The Indian Affair* (New York: Friendship Press, 1974), 62.

104. Ibid., 67.

105. Ibid., 68.

106. Ibid.

107. Vine Deloria Jr. to Donna Crossland, November 29, 1974. Author has copy of letter.

108. Ibid., 2.

109. Ibid., 3.

110. Ibid.

111. Ibid.

112. Ibid.

113. "Interior Department Releases 2015 Status Report for Land Buy-Back Program, Announces New Initiative to Expand Implementation Schedule," News Release, November 4, 2015.

114. "Of Indians," *Akwesasne Notes* (Early Winter 1975) (reprinted Mid-Winter 1985): 22.

115. Ibid.

116. Ibid., 23.

117. Ibid.

118. Ibid., 23.

119. Ibid.

120. *Los Angeles Times*, August 17, 1975, part IV, p. 5.

121. Ibid.

122. Vine Deloria Jr., "The Twentieth Century," in *Red Men and Hat Wearers: Viewpoints in Indian History*, ed. Daniel Tyler (Fort Collins: Colorado State University, 1976), 155–166.

123. Ibid., 163.

124. Vine Deloria Jr., "The Western Shoshone," *American Indian Journal*, vol. 2, no. 1 (January 1976): 20.

125. For an analysis of the ICC, Court of Claims cases, and other Indigenous claims against the United States. see David E. Wilkins, *Hollow Justice: A History of Indigenous Claims in the United States* (New Haven, CT: Yale University Press, 2013).

126. Vine Deloria Jr., *A Better Day for Indians* (New York: The Field Foundation, 1977), 7.

127. Ibid.

128. Ibid., 9.

129. Ibid., 10.

130. See, e.g., W. Dale Mason, *Indian Gaming: Tribal Sovereignty and American Politics* (Norman: University of Oklahoma Press, 2000); Paul Pasquaretta, *Gambling and Survival in Native North America* (Tucson: University of Arizona Press, 2003); Kenneth N. Hansen and Tracy A. Skopek, *The New Politics of Indian Gaming* (Reno: University of Nevada Press, 2011); and Katherine Spilde and Jonathan B. Taylor, "Economic Evidence of the Effects of the Indian Gaming Regulatory Act (IGRA) on Indian and Non-Indian Communities," *UNLV Gaming Research and Review Journal*, vol. 17, no. 2 (Spring 2013): 13–30.

131. Ibid., 77–33.

132. Ibid., 34.

133. 96 Stat. 2515, 2517.

134. Ibid., 2517.

135. *Hodel v. Irving*, 481 US 704 (1987); see also *Babbitt v. Youpee*, 519 US 234 (1997).

136. 99 Stat. 3171 (1984); 105 Stat. 1908 (1991); and 114 Stat. 1992 (2000).

137. 592 F.2d 575 (1st Circ. 1979).

138. Vine Deloria Jr., from typed transcript of trial, *Mashpee Tribe v. New Seabury Corp.* Author has copy of transcript.

139. Ibid.

140. Ibid.

141. 72 Federal Register 8007.

142. Vine Deloria Jr., "Traditional Indian Position Paper" (unpublished, 1977). Not paginated. Author has copy of document.

143. Congress attached a rider to an Indian Appropriation Act in 1871 that said that "hereafter no Indian nation or tribe within the territory of the United States shall be acknowledged or recognized as an independent nation, tribe, or power with whom the United States may contract by treaty: Provided, further, That nothing herein contained shall be construed to invalidate or impair the obligation of any treaty heretofore lawfully made and ratified with any such Indian nation or tribe" (16 Stat. 544, 566).

144. V. Deloria, "Traditional Indian Position Paper."

145. Ibid., 9.

146. Chief Irving Powless Jr. to Richard Moe Esquire, February 4, 1977. Author has copy of letter.

147. Vine Deloria Jr. "…But What of Human Rights for US Indians," *Los Angeles Times* (August 7, 1977), p. E3.

148. Ibid.

149. 448 US 371 (1980).

150. Vine Deloria Jr., "Like the Victory Over Custer, the Sioux's Legal Win Can Mean Defeat," *Los Angeles Times* (July 6, 1980), p. D1

151. Ibid., 2.

152. Ibid.

153. Ibid.

154. Raymond I. Orr, *Reservation Politics: Historical Trauma, Economic Development, and Intratribal Conflict* (Norman: University of Oklahoma Press, 2017), 4.

155. Vine Deloria Jr. to John Petoskey, November 7, 1983. Author has copy of letter.

156. "Future Strategies," *Indian Truth*, no. 255 (February 1984): 9.

157. Ibid.

158. Vine Deloria Jr. and Clifford M. Lytle, *American Indians, American Justice* (Austin: University of Texas Press, 1983), 106–107.

159. 114 Stat. 46.

160. Vine Deloria Jr. and Clifford M. Lytle, *The Nations Within: The Past and Future of American Indian Sovereignty* (New York: Pantheon Books, 1984), 245.

161. Ibid., 255.

162. Ibid., 258.

163. Ibid., 260.

164. James B. Reed and Judy A. Zelio, comps. and eds., *States and Tribes: Building New Traditions* (Washington, DC: National Conference of State

Legislatures, 1995). And see Andrea Wilkins, *Fostering State-Tribal Collaboration: An Indian Law Primer* (Lanham, MD: Rowman & Littlefield Publishers, 2016).

165. Washington State was the first to forge such an accord with many Native nations in 1989. Called the Centennial Accord, it has led to improved, although far from perfect, relations between the parties. More recently, see the Executive Order establishing a similar arrangement between the eleven federally recognized Dakota and Anishinaabe nations in Minnesota and Governor Mark Dayton, signed in 2013.

166. Deloria and Lytle, *The Nations Within*, 260.

167. Vine Deloria Jr. and Sandra L. Cadwalader, *The Aggressions of Civilization: Federal Indian Policy Since the 1880s* (Philadelphia: Temple University Press, 1984).

168. 60 Stat. 939.

169. Vine Deloria Jr., "Congress in Its Wisdom: The Course of Indian Legislation," in Deloria and Cadwalader, *The Aggressions of Civilization*, 127.

170. US Senate. Hearing Before the Select Committee on Indian Affairs. "Iroquois Confederacy of Nations." 100th Cong., 1st Sess., on S. Con. Res. 76 (Dec. 2, 1987).

171. Ibid., 24.

172. Ibid., 25.

173. Ibid.

174. Personal correspondence, April 7, 1988.

175. Ibid.

176. Ibid.

177. Ibid.

178. *United States v. Winans*.

179. *Winters v. US*.

180. *Quick Bear v. Leupp*.

181. *Lone Wolf v. Hitchcock*.

182. *U.S. v. Kagama*.

183. Personal correspondence, June 17, 1988.

184. Personal correspondence, August 16, 1989.

185. Ibid.

186. Ibid.

187. Ibid.

188. Ibid.

189. National Indian Policy Center, "Report to Congress: Recommendations for the Establishment of a National Indian Policy Center" (Washington, DC: 1992).

190. US Senate. Hearing Before the Select Committee on Indian Affairs. "National Indian Policy Research Institute," 102nd Cong., 2nd Sess. (July 21, 1992), 94.

191. *Pro-Football, Inc., v. Harjo*, 567 F. Supp. 2d 46 (2008).

192. Ian Shapira and Ann E. Marimow, "Redskins Prevail in Long Fight over Name," the *Washington Post*, June 29, 2017.

193. 73 F.3d 982 (1995).

194. 163 US 504 (1896).

195. *United States v. Winans*, 198 US 371 (1905); *Winters v. United States*, 207 US 564 (1908); and *Tulee v. Washington*, 315 US 681 (1942).

196. Personal correspondence, January 5, 1996.

197. Ibid.

198. Personal correspondence, January 9, 1996.

199. National Congress of American Indians, Supreme Court Project, http://www.ncai.org/initiatives/supreme-court-project.

200. Vine Deloria Jr. to Robert G. Griffen, September 24, 1997. Author has copy of letter.

201. Ibid.

202. This quote derives from an article by Douglas Preston titled "The Lost Man" that was published in *The New Yorker* on June 16, 1997.

203. Vine Deloria Jr. to Robert G. Griffen, US Army Corps of Engineers, September 24, 1997. Author has copy of letter and report.

204. Ibid., 2.

205. Ibid., 8.

206. V. Deloria and Lytle, *Tribes, Treaties, and Constitutional Tribulations*, 161.

207. Vine Deloria Jr., "Thirty Years of Literature and Counting," interview with Vine Deloria Jr., by MariJo Moore, *News From Indian Country* (2000).

208. Vine Deloria Jr., "Vine Deloria," in Serle L. Chapman, ed., *We The People: Of Earth and Elders, Volume II* (Missoula, MT: Mountain Press Publishing Co., 2001).

209. Ibid., 291.

210. Ibid., 292.

211. See Wilkins, *Hollow Justice*, especially Chapter 7, "The *Cobell* Trust Fund Litigation and Settlement: An 'Accounting Coup,'" for a detailed assessment of this important lawsuit.

212. "Statement of the President on the Settlement of Cobell Class-Action Lawsuit on Indian Trust Management." Author has copy of the statement.

213. "Statement of Ken Salazar, Secretary of the Interior, on Proposed Settlement of *Cobell v. Salazar* before the Committee on Indian Affairs, United States Senate," December 17, 2009. Retrieved from indian.senate.gov/public/_files/KenSalazartestimony.pdf.

214. Heidi Bell Gease, "Deloria Says Indians, Whites Face Same Crises," *Rapid City Journal* (May 18, 2001).

215. Ibid.

216. Personal correspondence, April 14, 1987.

217. Ibid.

218. Deloria and Wilkins, *The Legal Universe*, 7.

219. Ibid.

220. Ibid., 8–9.

221. Ibid., 374.

222. Ibid., 375.

223. Ibid.

224. US Senate. Hearing Before the Subcommittee on Constitutional Rights of the Committee on the Judiciary. "Constitutional Rights of the American Indian." 89th Cong., 1st sess., on S. 961, S. 962 (June 22, 1965), 195.

225. Ibid.

226. Ibid.

227. Deloria, *Custer Died for Your Sins*, 95.

228. Ibid.

229. Vine Deloria Jr. to Robert Lane, May 29, 1969. Author has copy of letter.

230. NCAI is the largest and oldest intertribal interest group. In recent years, it has worked closely with its member tribal nations, the academic and scientific communities, and Congress and relevant federal agencies to help put into place policies and procedures, such as Institutional Review Boards, that enable Native governments to more carefully assess the kinds of research projects that might impact their communities, while at the same time providing guidance on parameters to those interested in researching Native peoples.

231. Ibid., 238.

232. See, for example, Matthew L. M. Fletcher's *American Indian Tribal Law* (New York: Aspen Publishers, 2011), which was one of the first books to detail the growth and jurisdictional authority of Native court systems. And consult works by John Borrows, a Canadian Anishinaabe, who has

written a great deal about Indigenous legal norms and traditions and how these can form a powerful foundation for cultural regeneration and for improved interactions with provinces and the Canadian state. See especially *Freedom and Indigenous Constitutionalism* (Toronto, Canada: University of Toronto Press, 2016) and *Drawing Out Law: A Spirit's Guide* (Toronto, Canada: University of Toronto Press, 2010). Christine Zuni Cruz is also doing important work in the area of cultural competence and literacy and seeing how that can and should be the foundation upon which to construct Native legal systems, child welfare programs, etc.; see "Toward a Pedagogy and Ethic of Law/Lawyering for Indigenous Peoples," vol. 82, *North Dakota Law Review* (2006).

233. Ibid., 232.

234. Ibid., 239.

235. The Confederated Tribes of the Colville Reservation, https://www.colvilletribes.com/.

236. Island Enterprises Inc., www.islandenterprisesinc.com.

237. Ibid., 251.

238. Vine Deloria Jr. to Bufort Wayt, March 30, 1970. Author has copy of letter.

239. Vine Deloria Jr. to Martin Burkenroad, April 29, 1970. Author has copy of letter.

240. There is a current national Indian interest group, the National Council of Urban Indian Health, that is devoted to working on the health concerns of Natives in a number of major metropolitan areas.

241. See, for example, Terry Straus, ed. *Native Chicago*, 2nd ed. (Chicago: Albatross Press, 2002); Myla Vicenti Carpio, *Indigenous Albuquerque* (Lubbock: Texas Tech University Press, 2011); and Evelyn Peters and Chris Anderson, eds. *Indigenous in the City: Contemporary Identities and Cultural Innovation* (Vancouver: UBC Press, 2013).

242. Vine Deloria Jr. to Leonard Bearking, no date. Author has copy of letter.

243. Vine Deloria Jr. to Sylvie Brachet, December 22, 1970. Author has copy of letter.

244. Ibid.

245. Vine Deloria Jr. to Karen (no last name), August 29, 1971. Author has copy of letter.

246. Ibid.

247. Ibid.

248. Vine Deloria Jr., "This Country Was a Lot Better Off When the Indians Were Running It," *The New York Times Magazine* (March 8, 1970): 244.

249. Vine Deloria Jr., "The American Indian and His Commitments, Goals, Programs: A Need to Reconsider," *The Indian Historian*, vol. 5, no. 1 (Spring 1972): 9.

250. Vine Deloria Jr. to Randolph L. Peters, September 7, 1972. Author has copy of letter.

251. Ibid.

252. Ibid.

253. Ibid.

254. Ibid.

255. Ibid.

256. See Warrior, *Tribal Secrets*, 40.

257. See, e.g., Vine Deloria Jr., *Legislative Analysis of the Federal Role in Indian Education,* Report prepared for the Office of Education, Department of Health, Education and Welfare (Washington, DC: 1975: *Indian Education in America: Eight Essays* (Boulder, CO: American Indian Science and Engineering Society, 1991); and with Daniel Wildcat, *Power and Place: Indian Education in America* (Golden, CO: Fulcrum Publishing, 2001).

258. Vine Deloria Jr. to Elaine R. Cummings, June 22, 1970. Author has copy of letter.

259. Deloria, "The American Indian and His Commitments," 9.

260. Ibid.

261. Vine Deloria Jr. to Charles E. Heerman, December 3, 1972. Author has copy of letter.

262. Ibid.

263. Ibid.

264. Ibid.

265. Ibid.

266. Vine Deloria Jr., "The Indian World Today," *American Indian Culture Center Journal*, vol. 4, no. 1 (Winter 1973): 4.

267. Ibid.

268. Vine Deloria Jr., "The Great 1974 Indian Budget Log-Jam," interview with Vine Deloria Jr., by Laura Wittstock, *Indian Voice*, vol. 3, no. 4 (June/July 1973): 8–10, 55–60.

269. Ibid., 10.

270. Ibid.

271. Ibid., 55.

272. Ibid., 56.

273. Ibid.

274. Ibid.

275. Deloria, "The Next Three Years," 27.

276. Ibid., 53.

277. Vine Deloria Jr., "Religion and Revolution Among American Indians," *Worldview*, vol. 17, no. 1 (January 1974): 15.

278. Ibid.

279. Ibid.

280. Ibid.

281. Ibid.

282. Vine Deloria Jr., "The Indian Movement: Out of a Wounded Past," *Ramparts*, vol. 13 (March 1975): 31.

283. Deloria, *The Indian Affair*, 80.

284. Deloria, "The Twentieth Century," 163.

285. Vine Deloria Jr., "A Conversation with Vine Deloria Jr.," (1977), interview by Steve Crum, Geraldine Keams, and Steve Nelson, *Sun Tracks*, vol. 8 (1978): 85.

286. Vine Deloria Jr. to Pierre Dommergues, May 28, 1973. Author has copy of letter.

287. Vine Deloria Jr., "Legislation and Litigation Concerning the Indians," *Annals of the American Academy of Political and Social* Science, vol. 436 (March 1978): 96.

288. Ibid.

289. US House. "Needs of Elementary and Secondary Education in the 1980s: A Compendium of Policy Paper." Committee on Educational Labor, 96th Cong., 2nd Sess. (January 1980), 654.

290. Ibid., 656.

291. Philip S. Deloria, "The Era of Indian Self-Determination: An Overview," in Kenneth R. Philp, ed. *Indian Self-Rule: First-Hand Accounts of Indian-White Relations from Roosevelt to Reagan* (Salt Lake City, UT: Howe Brothers, 1986), 200.

292. Vine Deloria Jr., "Landlord to Welfare Client: The Decline of the Indian in National Consciousness," *Humboldt Journal of Social Relations*, vol. 10, no. 1 (Fall–Winter 1982–83): 125.

293. Ibid.

294. Ibid., 127.

295. Vine Deloria Jr., "Education and Imperialism." *Integrateducation*, vol. 19 nos. 1–2 (1982): 58–63.

296. Ibid., 61.

297. Ibid.

298. Ibid.

299. Ibid., 62.

300. Vine Deloria Jr., *Social Science Journal*, vol. 19, no. 3 (July 1982): 1–8.

301. See, e.g., Daniel McCool, Susan M. Olson, and Jennifer L. Robinson, *Native Vote: American Indians, the Voting Rights Act, and the Right to Vote* (New York: Cambridge University Press, 2007); American Civil Liberties Union, "Voting Rights in Indian Country: A Special Report of the Voting Rights Project of the ACLU" (Atlanta: ACLU Voting Rights Project, September 2009); David E. Wilkins and Heidi K. Stark, *American Indian Politics and the American Political System*, 3rd ed. (Lanham, MD: Rowman & Littlefield Publishers, 2011), see especially Chapter 7, "Indian Political Participation: Patriotism, Suffrage, and Partisanship"; Pamela S. Karlan, "Lightning in the Hand: Indians and Voting Rights," *The Yale Law Journal*, vol. 120 (2011): 1421–1453; Jeonghun Min and Daniel Savage, "The Influence of Socio-Economic Characteristics on the Political Attitudes of American Indians," *The Social Science Journal*, vol. 49 (November 2012): 494–501; and Jean Schroedel and Ryan Hart, "Vote Dilution and Suppression in Indian Country," *Studies in American Political Development*, vol. 29 (April 2015): 40–67.

302. Deloria and Lytle, *American Indians, American Justice*, 123.

303. Deloria and Lytle, *The Nations Within*, 242.

304. Ibid., 243.

305. Ibid., 244–267.

306. Personal correspondence, July 11, 1987.

307. Ibid.

308. Vine Deloria Jr., "Out of Chaos," *Parabola*, vol. 10, no. 2 (Spring 1985): 22.

309. Ibid.

310. Ibid.

311. Personal correspondence, March 5, 1990.

312. Personal correspondence, March 13, 1990.

313. Ibid. Deloria eventually did write his family's genealogy in the book *Singing for a Spirit: A Portrait of the Dakota Sioux* (Santa Fe, NM: Clear Light Publishers, 2000); see especially "Part I: A Vision and a Prophecy." In a short afterword, Deloria pointedly noted that "there is no question that Christianity served as a bridge to enable the Sioux people to make the transition from their life of freedom to a new life confined within the small boundaries of the reservation. In spite of modern popular political

doctrines, there should be little doubt that many Sioux embraced Christianity when their traditional social institutions and the practice of their own religion were prohibited to them. The men's and women's societies of the old days continued as part of the new religious life of the people. Meetings featured traditional oratory as people debated programs for their societies for the coming year. Kinship responsibilities did not falter as people accepted the new religion. The better families followed most of the old ways and kept track of the relatives, although with intermarriage with non-Indians and people from other tribes, kinship also began to falter and accommodations had to be made. It should be clear from the Black Elk literature and other works, and from my grandfather's [Philip Joseph] discontent in his later life, that Christianity did not replace the old Sioux beliefs and practices. The core of the traditional religious ways continued to provide a foundation upon which another religious tradition could be seen to be useful for short time. Thus the current interest in traditional Sioux ways is not in any way a contradiction" (p. 216). While not a pronouncement of his own decision to practice traditional ways or give up on Christianity, this statement does reveal a man who had profound respect for the traditional ways and values of his nation.

314. Vine Deloria Jr., *Indian Education in America: Eight Essays* (Boulder, CO: American Indian Science and Engineering Society, 1991).

315. Vine Deloria Jr. and Daniel R. Wildcat, *Power and Place: Indian Education in America* (Golden, CO: Fulcrum Publishing, and the American Indian Graduate Center, 2001).

316. Deloria, *Indian Education in America*, 48.

317. Ibid., 50.

318. Ibid., 67.

319. Personal correspondence, May 12, 1995.

320. Vine Deloria Jr., "Rethinking Tribal Sovereignty," *American Indian Research & Policy Institute* (May 25–26, 1995, St. Paul, MN, 1995), 7.

321. Personal correspondence, April 22, 1997.

322. Ibid.

323. Vine Deloria Jr., "Intellectual Self-Determination and Sovereignty: Looking at the Windmills in Our Minds," *Wicazo Sa Review* (Spring 1998): 25.

324. Ibid., 27.

325. Ibid., 30.

326. Moore interview, "Thirty Years of Literature and Counting," 3a.

327. K. Marie Porterfield, "Vine Deloria Urges Indian Authors to 'Earn Their Spurs,'" *Indian Country Today* (May 31, 2000): LT2.

328. Vine Deloria Jr., interview with Vine Deloria Jr., by Derrick Jensen, *The Sun*, issue 295 (July 2000): 4–13.

329. Ibid., 13.

330. Deloria, "Vine Deloria Jr.," in *We, The People*, 293.

331. Richard A. Grounds, George E. Tinker, and David E. Wilkins, eds. *Native Voices: American Indian Identity and Resistance* (Lawrence: University Press of Kansas, 2003).

332. Vine Deloria Jr., "The Passage of Generations," in Grounds, Tinker, and Wilkins, *Native Voices*, 318.

333. Ibid., 320.

334. Ibid., 321.

335. Ibid., 323.

336. Ibid.

337. Vine Deloria Jr., *The World We Used to Live In: Remembering the Powers of the Medicine Men* (Golden, CO: Fulcrum Publishing, 2006), xvi.

338. Ibid., xv.

339. Ibid.

340. Vine Deloria Jr., *C. G. Jung and the Sioux Traditions: Dreams, Visions, Nature, and the Primitive* (New Orleans: Spring Journal Books, 2009). Edited by Philip S. Deloria and Jerome S. Bernstein.

341. Ibid., 7.

342. Ibid., 148.

343. Ibid.

344. Ibid.

345. Ibid., 149.

346. Ibid.

347. Ibid., 7.

348. Ibid.

349. David H. Getches to University of Colorado Board of Regents, November 11, 2003. Author has copy of letter.

350. Ibid.

351. Associated Press, "Timeline: Colorado Recruiting Scandal," ESPN, http://www.espn.com/college-football/news/story?id=1803891.

352. Vine Deloria Jr. to Elizabeth Hoffman, May 21, 2004. Author has copy of letter.

353. Ibid.

354. Vine Deloria Jr. "Vine's Projects," n.d. Author has copy of document.

355. Ibid.

356. Ibid.

357. Ibid.

358. Ibid.

359. Ibid.

INDEX

Please note that page numbers with *n* indicate notes; page numbers with *t* indicate tables.

About the Authors

David Wilkins

David E. Wilkins is a citizen of the Lumbee Nation and holds the McKnight Presidential Professorship in American Indian Studies at the University of Minnesota. Wilkins is the author or editor of a number of books, including *Dismembered: Native Disenrollment and the Battle for Human Rights*, which he coauthored with Shelly Hulse Wilkins. His articles have appeared in a range of social science, law, history, and ethnic studies journals.

Bobby Bridger

Bobby Bridger is renowned for "A Ballad of the West," his epic trilogy about the American West from the era of mountain man Jim Bridger to the closing of the frontier. Bridger's career in show business spans the rockabilly to "Music City, USA" era in Nashville, the cosmic cowboy scene in Austin, the flowering of folk music, and even Broadway theater. He is the 2016 recipient of the Neihardt Foundation's prestigious Word Sender award.

Sam Scinta

Sam Scinta is the former publisher of Fulcrum Publishing and worked with Vine Deloria Jr. for more than a decade. He is currently the founder and president of IM Education, Inc., an educational nonprofit, and a lecturer in political science at the University of Wisconsin – La Crosse.